L. van der Pijl

Principles of Dispersal
in Higher Plants

With 26 Figures

Springer-Verlag Berlin · Heidelberg · New York 1969

Dr. LEENDERT VAN DER PIJL
emeritus Professor of Botany, University of Indonesia
Visiting Professor at University of Nijmegen
Sportlaan 236, The Hague/Netherlands

The use of general descriptive names, trade marks, etc. in this publication, even if the former are
not especially identified, is not to be taken as a sign that such names, as understood by the Trade
Marks and Merchandise Marks Act, may accordingly be used freely by anyone. Title-No. 1540

Preface

The work offerred here is a companion volume to the work by K. FAEGRI and L. VAN DER PIJL "Principles of pollination ecology", which deals with the preceding phase of reproduction in plants.

In the present work too, the emphasis is on principles and ecology. It is neither an enumeration of mechanisms, nor a compilation of cases. RIDLEY's monumental work "The dispersal of plants throughout the world" already comprises 700 large pages of small print, and research has proceeded since then. Though this work is more than just a compilation and contains much insight and thoughts on principles in addition to reviews, its completeness hinders its use as a textbook. As a reference work, it is unsurpassed and the writer made frequent use of it.

The writer paid special attention to functional backgrounds for the use of taxonomists working with "characters" and to biosystematics at the macro-level.

He is indebted to Dr. P. MÜLLER-SCHNEIDER (Chur, Switzerland) for the permission to translate parts of his "Verbreitungsbiologie der Blüten-pflanzen" — of which permission a modest use has been made. Thanks are also due to the Director of the Rijksherbarium at Leyden, and to its librarian for the use of the library.

Mr. F. J. NATAN was so kind as to make a number of photographs at the author's wishes.

Prof. Dr. H. F. LINSKENS stimulated the work actively and made completion possible with the collaboration of the members of his staff at Nijmegen University, amongst which Miss I. DE ROOS should be thanked especially.

Dr. B. J. D. MEEUSE (Seattle) was of great service, criticizing the manuscript.

The Hague, summer 1968   L. VAN DER PIJL

Contents

I. Introduction

A. The Place of Dispersal in the Chain of Life

Microbiologists' concepts are seldom concerned with dispersal and areas of distribution. One of their rules, sometimes indicated as "Beijerinck's law", states: everything is everywhere, but the milieu (environment) selects. In microbiological terms, this means that a special substrate can demonstrate the presence, and promote the development, of certain microbes specialized for that substrate. Such lower organisms are evidently so easily spread that they are in principle not limited by the dispersal factor. Some fungi and mosses requiring special substrates (e. g., dung in the case of fungi) already advanced far, developing devices for directed transport of spores to preferred substrates; and, in the final analysis, higher plants did the same with their microspores (brought to the stigma) when the spores had lost their general dispersal-function. This directed transport of microspores is dealt with in pollination ecology. In higher plants, dispersal is a factor limiting distribution more severely.

In this book, we have to study the ways and means which the higher plants employ to reach, with their newly developed dispersal organs, sites where a new generation can be established. More specifically, this involves the methods used to keep their descendants separated in space and to provide each with its own site, where it can compete with other plants; it also concerns the methods employed to defend the future of the species by exploring new territories, or conversely to maintain a foothold on a favourable site.

Another feature of spores, the power to withstand and survive unfavourable conditions over a long time-span, also became manifest in the reproduction organs of higher plants. The products of these organs, such as the seeds, may combine the effect of genetic variation with dormancy, in contrast to vegetative resting organs which merely continue the life of the individual without hope for the future of the species in a changing environment.

In the present study, we shall have the opportunity to emphasize two different aspects, viz. actual dispersal as studied in the field, and the structural basis needed to attain this dispersal; both will be considered in an ecological context. All too often, the second aspect predominated so strongly in works on dispersal that they remained examples of herbarium-ecology, or worse, desk-ecology. Nevertheless, the structural aspect cannot be dismissed as the starting point, the more so since a mere enumeration of findings in certain sites (as in HEINTZE, 1932) produces an unmanageable chaos.

We must be aware of the fact that dispersal is but one link in the continuity of life on earth, which is perpetual colonization. It starts with presentation of the units (including dehiscence and detachment), if possible at the right time and place, as a preparation for dispersal. This preparation also makes travel possible by providing physiological and structural protective devices. After travel comes settlement, not always by mere deposition, and germination. Only then does the question arise of a suitable substrate allowing establishment.

Each of these parts of the whole phenomenon can be the bottleneck, and in every plant community each of these can be dominating. As the various aspects of the overall process are also reflected in the structure of dispersal units (outside mere dispersal function), there is all the more reason to study them. Sometimes anti-dispersal mechanisms are important for homeostasis.

We shall see in detail in Chapters VI and VII, and elsewhere, how unsound it is, biologically speaking, to limit our attention to mere dispersal. All aspects intermingle and may change in importance during succession and evolution, so that in the dispersal organs we shall find traits relating to other spheres of life. We shall try to keep these various features apart.

I shall often avoid the trodden path of temperate ecology and refer to tropical phenomena. This in the first place to be more universal, but also to be more fundamental, since the impoverished temperate conditions which prevail for certain herbs and pioneer plants in temperate regions are not truly representative.

It is also necessary to point out here provisionally, that in seed plants the dispersal organs arise ontogenetically out of so-called sexual organs, the flowers, therefore still manifesting properties of the latter (see p. 13). When coining terms, it will prove important to reckon with these remnant-conditions.

The general effects of seed dispersal, discussed before, should be augmented by a newer aspect. Next to pollen transport, seed dispersal is the most important single factor promoting the gene flow in populations. GRANT (1958), for instance, has pointed to the effect of good dispersal on variability in populations of *Juniperus* in contrast to the situation in *Cupressus* species.

B. Limitations and Objections

Just as was the case with pollination-ecology (cf. FAEGRI and VAN DER PIJL, 1966), dispersal-ecology fell into discredit in the twentieth century for being partly the writing-desk ecology mentioned above. Many nineteenth century authors saw selective advantage in, and ascribed a dispersal function to, each and every detail of fruits. Some explained the distribution of plants only on this basis. I must, however, point out that the first composer of a systematic account of dispersal (HILDEBRAND, 1873) already warned against such simplification. So did KERNER.

Just as in floral ecology, the resistance of the time had many roots. One of the objections was based on the anti-Darwinian attitude of some morphologists and new physiologists, who preferred so-called antiteleological explanations from their own fields. GOEBEL was of the opinion that the morpho-physiological pluriformity as just given had obtained some function only secondarily, by "utilization". In the field of flower-structure his work on "Entfaltungsbewegungen" (1924) is full of antiteleological "proofs", nowadays mostly acknowledged as beside the point since the directed functional development has in many cases become clear. He stated that a few adaptations in fruits should be "killed", apparently as they did not lend themselves to be "explained away" as a mere repetition of unfolding movements.

Obviously influenced by his work on sea-dispersal, GUPPY (1906) was a strong advocate of utilization alone. He stated (p. 100—102): Nature has never concerned herself directly with providing means of dispersal; the sticky layer on some seeds exists for secretion; the dispersing agencies take advantage of certain characters developed for other reasons and thus representing results of history; the principles of evolution and adaptation rule the world except in dispersal.

I wish to remark that this concept, even though valid in some cases, does not represent the whole truth: the combination of various "usable characters", which we shall meet, points to development in a certain direction.

The other ideological basis for disbelief in adaptation was a somewhat supranatural belief in immaterial forces and "Gestalt-philosophy" behind form. This typological approach, often applied to flowers, did not find a fertile soil in dispersal organs.

Recently an attack on dispersal functions and adaptation was made from quite a different angle, namely by considering the fruit only as an organ for germination, this probably also for ideological reasons. GINDEL (1960) denied its function for dispersal, considering its attractiveness as accidental. The juicy fruit is, according to him, an organ which ensures continuing life at germination, so that it is imperative that it remain intact. Dead and infected fruits and loose seeds give, according to his experiments, poor germination. Dry fruits, obviously, were not taken into account. MAYER and POLJAKOFF (1963) have already criticized this queer concept.

Though RIDLEY (1930) and others have given us an abundance of cases of correlation between area extension and the presence or absence of dispersal mechanisms, many plant geographers are apparently so impressed by the discongruity between area extension and dispersal mechanims in other cases that they neglect dispersal entirely, even when discussing the migration of floras.

Illustrative are the writings of CROIZAT, who discusses distribution only, calling it, however, dispersal. Migration implies dispersal and this requires some mechanism.

We cannot discuss here the supposed migration routes suggested by plant geographers, and mainly based on comparative counts of species and genera; we shall also be reluctant to accept uncritically "land-bridges" and continental drift. Of necessity, however, some speculations will have to follow in the chapter on island floras. We shall remain silent on "age and area". The existence of development-centers of taxonomic groups with far-flung outposts implies dispersal. Outposts are not done away with by always interpreting them as relics.

Indeed, dispersal and its attendant phenomena require much more study, but what has been achieved up to now deserves a textbook, not only the jeremiad of WEBB (in HAWKES, 1966) that what statements there are, are cloaks for ignorance.

C. History and General Literature

The field of study was for a long time dominated by Scandinavians. LINNAEUS and some pupils already performed experiments, even feeding seeds to animals to study the results for the seeds. HOLMBERGER published in 1785 a "Theory on the dispersal of plants over the world" in which he already recognised the seven main dispersal-classes. The linnean concept of origin "ex unico loco" played a role herein. Much later, some Germans (SPRENGEL, KERNER) as well as DELPINO became interested. Also DARWIN, who even performed experiments on buoyancy and on germination of seeds transported on the feet of water-fowl. HILDEBRAND produced the first modern, comprehensive review. This was, curiously, in the same year (1873) that HERMANN MÜLLER produced his fundamental work on floral ecology, and about the same time that DELPINO published his important work on the latter topic.

KERNER VON MARILAUN published his experiments on various topics in 1863 and inserted them into a chapter of his large popular work "Pflanzenleben" (1891), translated as "Natural history of plants" (1896). The work of DELPINO (1870—1905) in carpobiology is so imbedded in existing foundations that it is now forgotten. The Scandinavian DAMMER (1892) coined many terms and produced (for Polygonaceae) the first paper on dispersal mechanisms within a family. SERNANDER (1901, 1906, 1927) inspired a number of pupils. His collection of carpologia is still kept in Uppsala.

HEINTZE (1932) started a handbook of which only two instalments appeared. Although he gives useful reviews of the history of terms, the book is brain-wrecking by its confused nature and inadequate references. RIDLEY consistently misspells his name as HEINITZ, which makes it easy in many books to see how much is borrowed from RIDLEY.

Of the later books, also written in German, mention should be made of ULBRICH (1928) and MÜLLER-SCHNEIDER (1955). The first is rather general and well-documented on mechanisms, the second more limited in pages and in scope, very European, though very readable and with a broad background. In English we possess only two general, popular American booklets. The first, by BEAL (1898), contains original contributions on a schoolbook-level, the second (MATHENY, 1931) could not be consulted.

Some books by GUPPY (1906, 1912, 1917) of a mixed nature contain important new observations on sea-dispersal, but betray here and there an amateurish concept of biology. The dispersal-bible by RIDLEY (1930) is a monument indispensable to any writer on the subject, also to the present author, as a reference book. In our book we will, for the sake of brevity, often suffice with a reference to RIDLEY, also for the older literature.

The French have to make do with a long series of journal papers by MOLINIER and MÜLLER (1938), the latter the same as MÜLLER-SCHNEIDER, often cited.

Russian botanists, during the last decades, have shown much interest in the field but mainly in fruit-systems, as far as can be judged. The book by LEVINA (1957) apparently summarizes data for national use.

Very old literature from the 18th century up to 1905 is collected in CAMPAGNA (1905); that of the period 1873—1890 very thoroughly in MACLEOD (1904). I shall concentrate here on literature that appeared after RIDLEY, or was not cited by him.

II. General Terminology

In the first place, we must consider the name of the phenomenon under discussion. "Dispersal" was indicated expressly for English use by RIDLEY. He defined it as the active (dynamic) process of transportation, differentiating it from the result it leads to: the passive (static) state of distribution. Unfortunately, this scientific distinction seems insufficiently reflected in colloquial English. JACKSON's glossary gives the two terms as synonyms. In other languages, too, common usage makes no sharp distinction between the comparable words, so that foreign terms came into scientific use. Though I often use it, I shall not promote the use of the term "dissemination" in English; this for reasons to be explained below, although the other terms may cause confusion. A study entitled "Ancient Dispersals" proved to deal with distribution, and a paper named "Distribution by Means of Bats" concerned dispersal.

Some American papers use the term "dispersion" which is simply incorrect, having an established other meaning.

The term dissemination was used by LINNAEUS for a part of the overall phenomenon, namely the act of discharge or liberation of the seeds. STOPP (1958 b) preferred it to the confusing German terms, as do the French and the Italians. He gives it a wider scope than just dispersal, including later processes. I can object to this widening only that the word dissemination refers to seeds, not to spores and vegetative diaspores. The term "propagation" also meets with objections.

"Migration" is wrong in this context, as it denotes in zoology the massdisplacement of a mobile, existing population. For long-term phenomena of shifting vegetations the use of this term may be continued in preference to "expansion".

Next come terms for the branch of science embracing our field, a question avoided in the title of this booklet. We shall see that "chorology" is the correct term, but unfortunately it seems to be pre-empted in current botany. "Dispersal-ecology" might form a parallel to "pollination-ecology". ULBRICH (1928) used as a subtitle "carpobiology", which is at the same time too wide and too narrow.

We have to move on to the smaller categories in our field, discussing the separate links of the over-all process. DAMMER (1892) used the suffix -chory (chorein = to wander) behind the name of the agent for classes of diaspores transported by this agent. This has been generally accepted and followers (such as NORDHAGEN) used the term "chorology" for the whole field of knowledge. Since RÜBEL (1920), however, the term has been usurped by plant-geographers for the knowledge of plant distribution, probably interpreting "chory" as derived from "place". BARKMAN (1958) used "chorology" broadly, subdividing it into four categories, according to static, dynamic, causal and historical aspects respectively, and placing dispersal in the second category.

The suffix -phily (= friend) will here, as usual, be combined with the same agents, to indicate the mode of transport of spores, especially microspores and their successors, the pollen grains. This transport of haploid dispersal units thus concerns the pollination-phenomena, starting in Pteridosperms.

The neutral suffix -phily emphasizes the specific dispersal to a "friendly" place, ultimately the stigma. Important aspects are its asexual character (despite LINNAEUS) and the morphological continuity of this spore-dispersal in lower and higher plants (cf. FAEGRI and VAN DER PIJL, 1966). A fungus, a moss, and a flower having their spores transported by wind, may all be called anemophilous.

Some terminological difficulty arises when isospores of lower plants are considered as merely serving the purpose of dispersal and falling under the -chory category. In these plants, -chory and -phily are not yet differentiated and may both be used, for instance "autochory" for a fungus or fern shooting its spores away. The undirected dispersal-element stands here in the foreground, even though one might point out that it is just the first step in the presentation to the wind, and also that the spore-dispersal is but the first step towards establishment of a new diplont. In old publications -phily was used for dispersal-categories, too; also in DANSEREAU and LEMS (1957).

The suffix -gamy (gamein = to marry) has to be reserved for purely sexual processes, such as the transport of and the differentiation between gametes. From algae up to some Gymnosperms we find their transport happening in water: hydrogamy. Later on, siphonogamy, porogamy, etc. arose. I must again admit a weakness in the lower regions of the plant kingdom. In algae, the transport of spores and that of gametes is not yet clearly differentiated in character, and consequently not in terminology. The French preference for -gamy in terms relating to flower pollination is perhaps understandable, but should be condemned as a linnean prematurity to the real sexuality. I have to admit that LINNAEUS was a native of Sweden who studied in Holland.

The suffix -spory points to some peculiarity of the diaspores.

Now that we have touched on national feelings it becomes necessary to proceed. In classification generally two different aspects can be emphasized, resulting in two approaches. One is the delimitation of classes to obtain a clearcut system with sharp boundaries. The other approach is to find common characteristics in a group, pointing to common relations to a certain factor. An ideal system uses dividing walls to separate, as well as nuclei to concentrate and to include — as in an organism. In German handbooks, the dividing walls are often stressed. In contrast, the Englishman RIDLEY had an aversion to classification and its terminology, claiming that terms are not essential and abandoning "dissemination" for the more vague term of dispersal. Although classifying his cases in orderly fashion, he denied that a natural category deserves a special term. In actual fact, the coining of terms makes the subject matter easy to handle, especially by resorting to the use of adjectives. E. g., one can time and time again speak about certain plants as having characteristics in their seeds or fruits which cause these to be regularly transported by ants. It is, however, simpler to say that such plants are myrmecochorous (a term especially despised by RIDLEY).

One might expect here definitions of the different organs of dispersal. However, I shall refrain from such definitions, as a thorough analysis of what constitutes an ovule, a seed, or a fruit in the different groups of seed plants, and an inquiry as to the origin of their constituent parts would lead to premature and out-of-the-way phylogenetical and morphological speculations. For the simple descriptive enumeration of fruit forms, I refer to morphological textbooks. We shall preferably restrict ourselves to functions and provisionally to classical ideas on carpels and ovaries, even though this field is in constant flux (MEEUSE, 1966).

In general, it seems superfluous to create terms for the units adapted to different agents of dispersal; in the following chapters, where we shall investigate how they function and how their structure is changed in time, the morphological terminology (which already has an ecological background) is usually sufficient. Terms for each functional modification in a morphological unit would result in chaos.

DANSEREAU and LEMS (1957) felt a need for some semi-functional system and for semi-functional names for diaspores when they constructed the dispersal-spectra used for describing communities. They created classes of diaspores based on apparent structure for dispersal, regardless of whether these would turn out to fulfill their "obvious" functions or not. Although this is not yet the occasion to criticize their system, I must point out that classes based on just one or two visible characteristics are far too simple for use in general ecology. The creation of such simple classes neglects colour, taste, smell, and the real function (as we shall see on p. 69), and does not reckon with arils or such important details as atelechory. The rather negatively defined group of the "sclerochores" of DANSEREAU and LEMS contains hydrochorous nutlets, myrmecochorous diaspores, mimetic diaspores, beans, beech-nuts, etc. For "barochores" see p. 76. The "ballochores" (diaspores forcibly ejected from the parent plant) are in reality very heterogeneous, as we shall demonstrate, and the characteristic structures are rarely situated on the diaspores, being usually present on organs of the mother plant.

A general nomenclatural objection, related to the last remark, is that terms pertaining to properties of diaspores (not directly to agents) should end with the suffix "-spore". CLEMENTS did so in his parallel terms for a comparable use as early as 1904 and 1905. I fear that the terms discussed may cause confusion with terms ending in -chory, which already exist in general dispersal ecology, and that there is considerable overlap. Further terms follow in our respective chapters. Readers overwhelmed by the multitude of names may perhaps be appeased when learning that inclusion of those used in the fruitsystems (to be discussed on p. 14) would have brought in several hundreds more.

III. The Units of Dispersal

Ever since SERNANDER, the plant part to be spread has been indicated, independently of its morphological value, as diaspore (from diaspeiro = I broadcast). Sometimes we find the terms propagule, germule, migrule, or disseminule. SERNANDER also gave a simple system, repeated here with some modifications. Its inadequacies will appear in the chapter on evolution. The system does not, of course, depend on function and agents, and is thus of little importance to us here.

A. Spores (in lower plants).

B. Haplonts (see Chapter VIII).

C. New diplonts with envelopes (usually indicated as generative units).
1. Nude embryo.
2. Nude seed by itself (primary and secondary gymnospermous plants, see p. 110).
3. Seeds liberated from dehiscent fruits (with or without arilloid).
4. Fruits. From one ovary (simple fruits) or from many ovaries in one flower (aggregate fruits).
5. Spurious (false) fruits or pseudocarps. From ovary plus other parts.
6. Multiple or collective fruits, from inflorescences (syncarps).
7. Seed contained in whole plant or part thereof (e. g. tumbleweeds).

D. Vegetative parts of the old diplont.

It seems necessary to discuss the types C-1 and D separately here and now.

The nude embryo seems, at first sight, theoretically important as a transition to types A and B. Scattering of embryos is said to occur in *Selaginella* and other higher Pteridophytes. However, this may be an incidental regressive adaption to water in the habitat, absent in Pteridosperms. Indeed, this is the situation in the aquatic Angiosperms to be discussed under hydrochory and vivipary (see RIDLEY p. 187), and also in seeds dispersed by water-animals (? *Inga*). In other cases (Loranthaceae c. s.) the useful presence of a testaless seed is perhaps the logical result of a reduction in the flower.

Vegetative Parts in Dispersal and False Vivipary

The role of vegetative parts will not come up in later chapters, so we must deal with it here in a definitive manner. For descriptive compilations see MÖBIUS (1940) and WEBER (1967).

I leave aside persistent subterranean parts that function only as a reserve for the individual plant and as survival organs for geophytes, though rhizomes and stolons may produce new individuals nearby and contribute to mass expansion of individuals arrived as seeds; they may provide definite settlement, even when sexual unbalance in a new habitat hinders seed formation. The floating away of torn-off rhizomes, as it occurs in many water- and beach-plants, can become the main, or sole, mode of dispersal. Such was the case with *Acorus calamus*, the sweet flag — which at an early date was introduced into Europe by man and is there sterile, due to triploidy.

In aquatic plants, fragmentation of stems and stolons can easily take over the dispersal function from seeds, as was the case in *Elodea canadensis* when introduced into Europe (one sex only introduced or maintained, and thus sterile) and in *Lemna* spp., where flowering is (? consequently) rare. In the tropics, well-known cases are *Pistia stratiotes* and *Eichhornia (Pontederia) crassipes* (the latter also sterile after introduction). Mass-transport of whole plants is frequent in the "sudd" of tropical regions.

In epiphytic plants the transport of branches has been observed for *Tillandsia usneoides* when birds used them as nest material (KUHLMANN and KÜHN, 1947). *Lemna* is vegetatively transported on the feet of waterbirds. Some cacti (jumping cholla) use epizoochorous fragments.

The distinction between vegetative parts serving for reserve and rest and those for dispersal is, of course, vague. Droppers or bulblets of bulbiferous plants can be established again at a distance after disturbance of the soil, for instance one caused by ploughing (GALIL, 1965, for *Allium ampeloprasum*).

Very frequent is the production of special, easily detached vegetative parts with a clear dispersal function. They are commonly indicated as bulbils, even though their morphology may be heterogeneous; often, they represent swollen roots with an adjoining axillary bud, as in *Ranunculus ficaria* (some tetraploid forms) where they are dispersed by rain-wash. The "bulbils" on the tip of the leaves of *Malaxis paludosa* are so small and undifferentiated that they have been indicated as foliar embryos.

Some bulbils are thrown by ballistic mechanisms *(Dentaria bulbifera)*.

The genus *Dioscorea* produces tuber-like bulbils, dispersed also by water. In Indonesia the genus *Globba* has some forest-species which rarely fruit, instead producing bulbils from axillary buds in the inflorescence.

When such detached bulbils have the character of young plants that sprout immediately, the term "vivipary" is often applied. Even ULBRICH and MÜLLER consider this as true vivipary in contrast to the early sprouting of seeds on the mother plant, to be described later in a special chapter (p. 95). I do not agree, considering it at the most as "false vivipary" for the following reasons. The limit between early and late sprouting bulbils is vague; all easily sprouting vegetative parts such as subterranean stolons and bulblets would also fall under the term, and thereby the possibility of comparison with viviparous animals (bearing sexual products) would be lost. Many plants with inflorescences bending down and producing plantlets on the soil would have to de described as viviparous, such as the *Chlorophytum* cultivated as a house plant, or tropical *Marica* and *Limocharis* species. The so-called viviparous ferns have no "-pary".

Well known cases of such bulbil-production are temperate *Allium* species, *Polygonum viviparum*, and *Poa alpina*. In *Poa* we find dispersal by wind, in *Polygonum* by birds that treat the bulbils as seeds (they are often found in the gizzards of grouse, *Lagopus,* which excrete them partly undamaged). In tropical regions, *Bryophyllum* bears them on leaves and *Agave* in the inflorescences. In the last two cases there is some comparability with true vivipary, as the effect is not just dispersal but fast establishment in a rainy period, as discussed on p. 96.

Fig. 1. Remusatia vivipara. Stalk with bulbils

Some water plants produce special, hardy, dormant buds sinking in the mud against wintertime for survival; these are indicated as gemmae, hibernacula, winter-buds, or turiones, and may assist dispersal by fragmentation. Species of *Utricularia, Myriophyllum, Potamogeton* show this, in the latter accompanied by low seed-production (MUENSCHER, 1936).

Typical dispersal-bulbils are produced by some tropical Araceae. In *Gonanthus pumilus* these bulbils have long hairs (anemochory), in *Remusatia vivipara* they are provided with hooks like a burr (see Fig. 1). In the latter case, the flowers have sterile pollen, at least in Java. The plant was found in isolated, oceanic Christmas Island, far south of Java.

In many cases (also in *Ranunculus ficaria*), we found a correlation between sterility and the presence of vegetative propagation. The latter cannot be described as just an incidentally discovered way out of the danger of the former. There may exist a direct physiological relation (? hormonal) between the two, with each as possibly primary, — as seen in species of *Allium* and *Agave,* where removal of bulbils in the inflorescence promotes the ripening of fruits. In the Irish potato the prevention of tuber development has the same effect on sexual organs. The reverse influence is more evident in *Lilium bulbiferum,* where bulbils arise in case of non-pollination of the flowers.

The genus *Oxalis* often produces small bulbs underground. In *O. cernua* these detach easily as hardy, seed-like bulbils. In the Mediterranean region this alloploid hybrid is sterile and moreover, only the short-styled form has been introduced, so that the bulbs must be responsible for its wide distribution there outside gardens. This seemed at first enigmatic since in Israel the plant is even found in rock-fissures, high above ground-level. GALIL (1967), however, described dispersal of the bulblets by mole-rats *(Spalax),* blind, burrowing rodents that construct underground "granaries" with food-reserves. Thus all classes of dispersing agents have now been found to be represented in bulbils.

We discussed the physiology of bulbils which is important for ecology. The physiological influence of temperature and day-length will be left out here, but often a clear regulative relation has been found with some extreme condition that antagonizes normal, sexual propagation. There is also some concurrence with apomixis and polyploidy. In addition to diploid *Poa alpina* some grasses of the genus *Deschampsia* show a tendency to bulbil-formation, increasing with the chromosome-number (FLOWIK, 1938).

We find one aspect of true seeds lacking in these cases, viz. the transport of a new genetic combination after recombination. This aspect is also absent in seeds originated after apogamy but we shall not discriminate against them in the following sections. It remains, moreover, questionable whether even nucellar embryony is purely asexual. Internal processes, including semi-meiotic nuclear processes, can provide genetic rearrangement and physiological restitution in the cell. The term "uniparental reproduction" seems more suitable here.

IV. The Relation between Flowers, Seeds and Fruits

A. Seed and Fruit

Since the rise of Pteridosperms, the seed has become the normal organ of generative, recombinative dispersal. Why then the fruit? In the chapter on evolution we shall see in detail that the fruit is in principle an interpolation, the continuation of a new organ of the flower, the ovary. This persisted after flowering and, after a phase where it was only a nuisance, it usually became an auxiliary organ of dispersal which supplanted the seed as such. Morphologically the difference between the two seems clear, the one arises from an ovule and the other from an ovary. Difficulties arise when we consider whether all ovaries are comparable or not, and whether perhaps some ovaries are homologous with seeds. As long as this does not involve ecology, we might leave these questions to morphologists, but this attitude becomes untenable when we realize that pure morphology is an abstraction, that morphology is perhaps the crystallized or fossilized ecology of former eras.

As long as we considered present temperate conditions as normal, basic and eternal, we had no trouble with the classical concepts mentioned, nor with those of fruit and seed. The seed then was assumed to be essentially small, hard, and dormant, finally liberated from the fruit. We shall have to discard such assumptions.

Such concepts but rarely ascribe an independent role in dispersal to the seed, although admitting such a role for small anemochorous, winged, or plumed seeds. In archaic and many tropical seed plants the seed still plays the more active role, described under evolution, with the intervening fruit secondarily repeating the functions and structures.

In our description of the ecological classes we can, therefore, also refrain from treating seed and fruit (and aggregates) separately in each chapter. A drupe and a berry repeat the functional structure of the seed of *Ginkgo, Cycas, Encephalartos,* and *Magnolia.* It is, therefore, illogical to speak (as is usually done) of the seed of *Cycas* as drupe-like. As I have said, considerations on homology in fruits and its precise analysis are for the time being superfluous in ecology, a discipline which works with convergent organs and tissues. The palisade layer of seeds is convergent. A drupe then answers the old description in the work of GAERTNER in 1788 on fruits, irrespective of the homology of juicy and protective parts. In an effort to bring in homology as a tool for defining fruit-classes in a system, TAKHTAJAN (1959) distinguished between drupes from inferior and superior ovaries. This is not only ecologically superfluous but also morphologically insufficient. Inferiority of the ovary is based on divergent morphological conditions (occlusion by either axis-parts or appendicular parts). And, worse, it is not "pure" morphology (if such morphology is possible at all), since inferiority is a convergent ecologism in the flower-phase.

B. Morphological Fruit Systems

In spite of these and other objections, various authors have considered it possible to construct systems of fruits on a morphological basis. Attempts were made by WINKLER (1939, 1940) and BAUMANN-BODENHEIM (1954). It has also been thought possible to construct systems on a double basis: viz. first the "general", "morphological", ecologically neutral basis of the carpels and their coherence, and secondly the refinements occasioned by the ecological requirements of dehiscence, consistency, etc. Many East-European systems reflect this attitude: GOBY (1921), GUSULEAC (1938), HEGEDÜS (1948), TAKHTAJAN (1959), and KADEN (1965). Worthy of special note is the system of LEVINA (1961). All these systems shower us with a deluge of new terms (hundreds) not to be cited here, and merely providing compilers of future glossaries with parkinsonian work. In the East-European systems, the morphological bases are indicated as "genetic", meaning in this world of thought "ontogenetical". The deeper morphology of the constructional parts in ontogeny is either neglected or considered at the classical level of Goethean simplicity and typology. The line of development described in them is typological on a basis of monophyletic angiospermy. To mention an instance, the disappearance of septa in monolocular fruits can just as well be read in the opposite sense or be explained on the basis of the revolutionary concepts of the New Morphology (MEEUSE, 1966).

C. Morphological Interaction between Fruit and Flower

1. General

Morphologists should be extremely careful when dealing with the fruit, the youngest organ, of an ecological nature, where function is dominant and causes endless convergence. I have other fundamental objections against the principle of adopting a morphological basis for fruit-systems. One is its inadequacy with regard to the pluriformity which exists in groups such as the Leguminosae (see Chapter IX), where the simple and uniform ovary produces a world of forms and where pure morphologists must feel like deaf people arguing about music.

Another objection ist that the fruit-morphology cited refers in essence to the ovary and thus to an organ of the flower, an organ for pollination not necessarily bound to functions of the fruit. I do not understand how ESAU, in her textbook of plant anatomy, could postulate that the classification of fruits should reflect the structure of the flowers. Flowers in what phase? The function of the flower in all stages, containing three generations (old diplont, haplont, and new diplont), is of a triple nature: first spore-production, then fertilization of the haplont with embryogenesis, then formation of seed and fruit. The different spheres of life remain in this contraction nevertheless more or less separate in their adaptations.

There is, however, interaction. The anatomy of the ovule can be influenced by the later function of the seed. A vascularization of the integument may be just a prelude to a special testa, such as the sarcotesta of Sapindaceae or the watery, viviparous testa of Hymenocallis (see p. 112 and p. 96). Often a mental analysis is necessary to decide for what sphere of life a constructional detail can be interpreted as adaptive and to which one it can be assigned in terminology. This differentiation in terms is not a mere play on words, but is necessary for the correct insight into the nature of things. The often-committed sin of interchanging terms for the flower and the fruit hinders, as will be shown, insight into the interaction and into the backgrounds of taxonomic and phylogenetic relations. We shall later see how misleading the unfortunate use of the seed-term angiospermy for the flower has been.

Some interaction between pollination and seed dispersal (between flower and fruit) seems, however, unavoidable in an organ serving both processes. BURTT (1961) indicated this interaction in the heads of Compositae, which also serve two functions, the pappus and involucrum being most active for fruiting. ZOHARY (1950) had already pointed to the two distinct evolutionary trends in them, as discussed under heterocarpy on p. 82. Where there is interaction, I shall indicate the influence of the flower-phase on the seed or fruit as postludial and the reverse, anticipative influence as preludial. Sometimes a fourth sphere of life, germination, can prelude in seed and fruit. I shall not complicate matters in ontogenetical sequence by considering the seed as prior to the flower in an evolutionary sense.

2. Position

The terminological differentiation of characteristics is evidently necessary in regard to the position, the place of presentation. We find a special position on the trunk and on dangling long stalks in bat-flowers (see FAEGRI and VAN DER PIJL, 1966) but also in bat-fruits (see p. 43). In flowers, we have to call the phenomena cauliflory and flagelliflory respectively, in fruits or seeds caulicarpy and flagellicarpy (flagellispermy). The interaction between the two is evident when there is no postfloral change in position (as indeed there is in the dangling seeds of *Swartzia* (p. 44) or in the dangling fruits of *Mangifera* of Fig. 12). Without this, one of the two spheres can dominate. The non-chiropterophilous flower can already, as a prelude to the cauli-carpous bat-fruit, be situated on the trunk, although at first sight this "does not seem to make sense". This is the case in *Ficus* spp. with archaic pollination by wasps, for whom the position is unimportant. The reverse is the case with the non-chiropterophilous fruit which as a postludium remains on the trunk when its flower was more or less cauliflorous for pollination by bats. This is presently the case in *Durio Zibethinus* where the fruit is dropped before dispersal, thus being non-functionally caulicarpous. The plant-species is cauliflorous. In *Artocarpus heterophylla* (jackfruit) we meet a convincing refinement. The position on the trunk concerns the female inflorescences only and appears thus as caulicarpy, for bat-dispersal.

The adaptive positioning of ant-fruits near the ground (see p. 49) can be performed by postfloral changes of the flower stalk, but can be preluded in the flower, as SERNANDER (1927) already remarked. He even found consequences of this in the flower of some species of *Geranium* and *Veronica*, i. e., in a reduction of cross-pollination correlated with a deviating fruit-ecology. In geoflory and geocarpy the changes in position between flower and fruit are better known. *Arachis* even shows two opposite elongations. The flowers, placed low, bring the attractive part of the flower upward by an extremely long hypanthium or perianth tube, quite exceptional in Papilionaceae. This tube wilts postflorally and the unstalked ovary now develops a stalk which pushes the fruit into the soil.

3. Monovuly and Monospermy

The number of seeds and ovules is subject to the interaction between flower and fruit. The reduction to one ovule has to be indicated as monovuly (as distinct from monospermy). It is adaptive for anemophily, very clearly so in families with habitual polyovuly and entomophily, where one species has become anemophilous and monovulous. Monospermy is clearly adaptive in plants with indehiscent dry fruits and drupes. It is one of the ways of escape from angiovuly (p. 109). In grasses monovuly and monospermy are both functional, the first seeming to be the primary one as a consequence of wind pollination (see FAEGRI and VAN DER PIJL, 1966).

In Fagaceae monospermy seems primary with regard to the production of nuts and acorns, monospermous fruits with large seeds, which have an adaptive value in the rain-forest (see p. 87). The correlative reduction of the ovule-number seems a preludial interaction. Primary monovuly seems excluded since the basic tropical oaks and chestnuts are still entomophilous (old cantharophily as described in FAEGRI and VAN DER PIJL). We may even assume that this secondary monovuly paved the way to later anemophily in temperate regions. We see that an adaptation in one field can start a new radiation in another field. The same path was probably followed in Polygonaceae and Compositae, as we shall see.

4. Inferiority and the Calyx

Inferiority of the ovary is usually a floral character. In many cases it has been explained functionally as a protective device against beetles, which were the pollinators in early periods. This may also be applied to the Compositae which arose in the beetle period. The reasoning cannot be applied to cases of a more recent character, such as in Ericaceae, where inferiority by occlusion of the ovary inside torus and calyx appears in the genus *Vaccinium*. The envelopment of the fruit proper by the calyx into a pseudoberry, so common in related genera, seems in *Vaccinium* to be anticipated in the floral phase.

In the Compositae too, however, we find as a first preludial influence of the later pappus the special transformation of the free calyx parts in the floral phase. A fuller indication of possible anticipation in their calyx follows on p. 130.

D. Inadequacy of Current Fruit-Terminology

Some fruit-systems deviate from those indicated as morphological. The one by JANNCHEN (1949) calls itself functional, thinking it unwise to place fruits in a morphological straitjacket, although using morphological criteria and tending to neglect dissemination.

The current terminology and the fruit-system used in handbooks and schoolbooks stem from extensive reviews as in the "Handwörterbuch der Naturwissenschaften" of which PASCHER and POHL revised the second edition (1934). It is, in principle, monstrous as it uses diverse criteria indiscriminately: morphological, ontogenetical, histological, ecological, and physiological. No wonder representatives of each of these branches have complained about the inconsistencies and inadequacies! The system characterizes anything that does not fit into it as "accessory". This comprises, as we shall see, a large part of archaic and tropical fruits. It is too European-centered, even in its terminology, focusing on pericarp fruits. STOPP (1950 and many subsequent papers) showed the insufficiency, but as yet no typological school has produced a complete system. I mentioned some, more morphological, systems before and must admit that I could not produce anything better if it were necessary in this book. The fruit is too versatile and has too many aspects to be divided into strict categories. We shall see this in the ecological part, but point already now to some types of true fruits that need recognition and perhaps a name:

a) Seeds dominating

1. Seeds attractive, pericarp early caducous
2. Seeds juicy, carpel opened early
3. Nude seeds dry, pericarp open as a dry wing
4. Sarcotesta seeds in dry pericarp
5. Seeds arillate, further ibidem

b) Seeds regressing, dry

6. Mesocarp hard, endocarp pulpous (partly under the hesperidium)
7. Mesocarp hard, endocarp dry, splitting off
8. Pericarp dry, placenta fleshy
9. Pericarp fleshy, dehiscing.

V. Ecological Dispersal Classes, Established on the Basis of the Dispersing Agents

A. General

The sequence in which the various classes in dispersal ecology are to be presented seems at first irrelevant, as each agent, in principle, has the same rights. The question arises, however, whether historically the different agents could and did exert their rights equally well. The sequence used in most handbooks, although neither logical nor historically correct, has found wide acceptance, so that I have to justify my own deviating order; the more so, as our chapter on evolution will prove the existence of a certain line of development, which does not start with the anemochory or autochory often assumed to be basic. In Pteridosperms and Gymnosperms we shall find reasons to consider dispersal of seeds by animals to be dominating. The wind-dispersal of some *Pinus* seeds is derived from the animal dispersal in large-seeded species. The concept of anemochory as basic goes back to SERNANDER (1927), who was probably misled by the prejudice of his time as well as by the special situation prevailing in Europe. Thus he was influenced by:

1. the onesidedness of European Gymnosperms, as anemochores;
2. the neglect of Ranales as primitive;
3. a false analogy between seeds and wind-dispersed spores;
4. the false concept of basic wind-pollination in Amentiferae and of the primitivity of this group;
5. the concept that small seeds are basic.

Autochory is clearly a late way out, of limited importance; to be sure, in discussions of the topic it is often placed in front, but this is done for nonbiological reasons (do-it-selfers first).

One might try to classify the subject-matter pertaining to dispersal on the basis of the diaspores of the plants, but this does justice neither to the convergent ways of nature nor to its complexity, as we saw when discussing diaspores. The only practical order is obtained by following RIDLEY, with the agent of transport as the criterion for the main classes. It should be remembered that in pollination-ecology the same order was recognized as correct after similar prejudices had been overcome.

As in pollination, we shall find for the classes a general set of characteristics called the syndrome, sometimes wide, sometimes narrow and precise. Again, as in pollination-ecology, not all the features are necessarily present, a single one sometimes being sufficient and decisive.

B. Invertebrates

Entomophilous fungi and mosses established a regular contact with flies transporting spores from one dung heap to another. In the disperal of the much larger seeds which appeared on the scene later, the role of insects is almost negligible, although incidental finds are reported. The exception is formed by ants, also late-comers, but the connection between seeds and these animals is so special and comes so clearly on top of older connections that we have to preserve it for the last, as an afterthought of nature.

The much older termites are purely dystrophic, meaning that they destroy anything transported, except fungus-spores. The data on *Rafflesia* seeds in this regard are for the time being mere presumptions.

Dung beetles in deserts contribute to germination by burying dung with seeds.

There exist old data on dispersal by snails, especially for strawberries. MÜLLER-SCHNEIDER (1955) paid some attention to this point, adding some cases of ornithochorous berries eaten by snails, a. o. tomatoes. Except the case of *Adoxa,* added later by him (1967), all this seems incidental utilization, without much dispersal value.

We must, however, after assistance by Dr. DOEKSEN (Wageningen) mention earth worms as dispersers. DARWIN already ascribed such a role to them. Seeds have been found inside them and are mostly defecated underground. Other old data, from BECCARI's book "Malesia", are not to be neglected. He suspected earth worms as dispersers of the small seeds of saprophytic orchids, Burmanniaceae, etc. I always wondered how saprophytic *Epirrhizanthes* proceeded to get its small seeds deep underneath the humus layer. The unconfirmed case of South-African *Isoetes* species, spread by spore-eating worms, is of theoretical interest as an ancient possibility. Worms may act as an intermediary agent, leading to further-distant dispersal when eaten by thrushes.

C. Fish

Vegetarian fishes may eat any botanical material, including seeds and fruits. Some seeds are even so attractive that they can be used as bait. The same is true for the sarcotesta-seeds of *Pithecellobium microcarpum* in

Borneo. A Brazilian, popular booklet by DE ARAGO (1947) describes how fishes (genera *Osteoglossum* and *Brycon*) are lured by fruits of trees growing on river shores. It gives only vernacular names of the trees but, as far as I could ascertain, these refer a. o. to the genera *Ficus, Inga, Myrciaria* (Myristicaceae), *Arecastrum* (Palmae) and *Guatteria* (Annonaceae). Many species of *Inga* prefer riverine habitats.

RIDLEY mentions *Pandanus helicopus* in this connection, and also mentions the seeds of *Nuphar luteum* and *Bombax munguba* as being eaten. CORNER (1940) mentions as eaten the pulpy seeds of *Dysoxylon angustifolium* and *Aglaia salicifolia* (Meliaceae), growing alongside rivers. The attention of fishermen is asked here as to the fate of the seeds inside.

All this may be merely incidental, the more so as we do not know if the seeds pass undigested in these and other cases. On the other hand, there may exist a natural and regular bond between fish and the swamp- and riverside plants mentioned, especially in the regularly inundated areas in Amazonia, where glaciation could not prevent the persistence of archaic conditions. HUBER (1910), who was the first to suggest this, found in the intestines of large vegetarian fishes piracanjuba *(Brycon)* and pacu *(Myloplus)* seeds and kernels of Palmae and species of *Lucuma* and *Alchornea*, the latter with sarcotesta. KUHLMANN and KÜHN (1947) also mentioned Brazilian palm-fruits, especially *Geonoma schottiana*, as a preferred food of and bait for those fishes; also the fallen pods and seeds of leguminous *Inga* species. The latter may, like some other cases, be archaic remnants. The same holds for the leguminous seed of *Eperua rubiginosa*, also used as bait in baskets. The tree grows along creeks in Surinam. Large fishes swim up when a pod explodes with a bang and swallow the large seeds. In the seeds (also in those of *Inga*) the testa seems attractive, not protective. Protection seems, moreover, superfluous in these, not truly hydrochorous but nevertheless water-dependent seeds.

The European literature is rather silent on natural botanical fish food, and some of it is inaccessible. The researches of HOCHREUTINER, often cited, are of little value. Carp are said to eat fruits of the hydrochorous grass *Glyceria*. HEINTZE (1927) reported diaspores of *Aponogeton, Nuphar, Najas marina, Zizania aquatica, Salacia grandiflora* and *Ficus tweediana* as being present in South-American fishes, and the olive-like fruits of a *Posidonia* (Naiadaceae) as being eaten by tuna fish in the Mediterranean. Some relations between seeds and fish can, as said before, be incidental and arisen secondarily. Some species from carnivorous groups of fishes may have switched to late fruits offered in their biotope. An instance is the silarid *Arius maculatus* in the Indonesian mangrove, which feeds on the fruits of *Sonneratia* (used as bait) and even got its native name from this tree. The same may refer to the fruits of *Genipa americana,* discussed on p. 118, and used as fish-bait.

D. Reptiles and Saurochory

Amongst modern reptiles few vegetarians are left; some turtles and tortoises, a few lizards. The famous Galapagos lizards may have been driven forcibly into this habit of saurochory, as DARWIN already described in his "Voyage of a naturalist". RIDLEY cited these and other cases, amongst which are *Genipa clusiifolia* (Rubiaceae), *Celtis iguana* (eaten by climbing iguanas) and the rather hard alligator apple *(Annona palustris)*, eaten by iguanas and alligators after having dropped off the tree. The latter also has sea-transport. KRAL (1960) reported the gopherberry (*Asiminia pygmaea*, Magnoliaceae) as being eaten by terrestrial gopher turtles.

Recently DAWSON (1962) described in detail the importance of such reptiles for cactus fruits in the Galapagos Islands, pointing especially to the germination which then rapidly ensues. The local tomato variety can in fact germinate only after passing through a tortoise, but not through other animals (RICK and BOWMAN, 1961).

The desert iguana eats whole plants indiscriminately. KLIMSTRA and NEWSOME (1960) found mature seeds in box turtles amongst others of species of *Rubus, Fragaria, Prunus, Polygonum, Vitis, Diospyros*, and *Morus*. They showed that the animals had a well-developed sense of smell and a special optical sensitivity for orange-red. A number of zoologists (WOJTUSIAK, GRANIT, WAGNER, NICKEL) confirmed this and elaborated upon it in work on the sense-physiology of reptiles. The sense of colour is weak in nocturnal reptiles.

Research in the Guyanas and Amazonia may reveal many more instances. I think especially of dropped *Inga* fruits. The seeds mentioned in all those cases are a secondary selection of what is at present offered and accessible; it may be theoretically important, as pointing to some archaism, that relatively so many "ancient" Ranales and Rosaceae are present on the list.

It may also be important that *Fragaria, Rubus* and *Rosa*, although taken by birds, are not typically ornithochorous (because they possess smell); in southern Europe and USA wild strawberries are popular with turtles. These can reach other fruits that are close enough to the ground.

As a syndrome of characteristics of reptile fruits, we can at this point already state that the fruits may be coloured, have a smell, and are often borne near the ground or dropped at maturity. A hard skin is no obstacle for turtles with sharp beaks.

For the Asiatic tropics we have only some vague indications and traces discovered by BECCARI (1890). He had reason to believe that the primitive sarcotesta seeds (near the ground) of the low swamp palm *Zalacca edulis* are not eaten only by rodents (as seen elsewhere) but also by varanes and turtles. On the authority of Dyak helpers, he assumed that the large and hard arillate fruits of *Durio testudinarum* in Borneo are eaten by turtles, a belief expressed in the name. The native name for this and other basicar-pous *Durio* species (durian kura-kura) points in this direction. Now such a vernacular name might just mean "unfit for humans", but the names for the different *Durio* species are too specific for that (KOSTERMANS, 1958). The specific native names (also referring to birds) cannot refer to just external likeness.

Should the Durian Theory (cf. p. 113) on primitive fruits be revised on a reptile footing? In this connection, the basal caulicarpy or basicaulicarpy (on the trunk near the ground) of *Durio testudinarum* can be seen as an adjustment to ground animals. Other archaic *Durio* species (as *D. oxleyanus* and *D. dulcis*) have axillar and simpler flowers, and drop their smelly fruits. On the ground these expose by gradual decay (cf. *Degeneria* p. 110) and by opening the edible coloured arillodes. This situation (KOSTERMANS, 1958) seems impossible to understand without ancient connections with ground animals, originally reptiles, now also mammals. The basicarpy appears to affect adversely the high-level pollination of some *Durio* species (by bats). In *D. testudinarum* such pollination has not become impossible, as Dr. J. A. ANDERSON (Kuching) wrote me, for in the area where this species occurs bats have been caught at the expected low levels in mist nets.

Sometimes such basicaulicarpy is described as just geocarpy, a term better reserved for other phenomena, with underground fruits (p. 79). The term basicarpy can also be applied to other general phenomena (p. 78) in herbs.

We shall discuss here other cases of comparable basicaulicarpy, also of long fruiting stalks creeping over the ground. The two conected phenomena occur combined in a number of old groups with primitive zoochorous fruits: Annonaceae, Flacourtiaceae, Sapindaceae, Dilleniaceae, Euphorbiaceae, Ster-culiaceae; also in members of the old genus *Ficus*, already abundant in the Cretaceous. In "geocarpous" species of *Ficus*, the syconia are indeed more or less underground, a situation which is not demanded by the particular mode of pollination (by primitive wasps). The low position of flowers and fruits stands also outside the pollination sphere in some species of *Baccaurea* (Euphorbiaceae), such as *B. parviflora*, and in some species of *Stelechocarpus* (Annonaceae). There, only the female flowers are basiflorous (a situation without pollination function); consequently, the fruit is basicarpous, a situation with a dispersal function. The *Artocarpus* mentioned on p. 16 may have also been saurochorous originally. The special position of their female flowers was stressed as early as 1910 by HABERLANDT in a note on p. 292 of his "Botanische Tropenreise". Some palms join in.

In a later chapter, dealing with the geocarpy of desert plants (p. 80), I shall mention the case of a *Cephaelis* which might belong here. It demon-strates the danger of descriptive, undiscriminating terminology without appeal to function!

A number of papers on saurochory by BORZI (a. o. 1911) were inaccessible to me.

We may expect no exo- (epi-)zoochory on smooth reptiles and thus the
phylogenetic emergence of burrs had to wait for furred animals and herbs.
These burrs are lacking in simple Ranales too. Further discussion of the
evolutionary aspects of the conditions just mentioned will have to wait for
the special chapter. Let us, however, point out that when we call this kind
of cauliflory archaic, this does not mean that it is restricted to unbranched,
simple trees; that it is archaic only in the meaning of "not to be understood"
(CORNER).

We enter here the more general field of zoochory, dispersal by animals.
Before we proceed with further classes, we must recognize that in the
question of transport, also the "how" and "where" count. All following
zoochorous classes can be subdivided by crosswise partitions as follows:

a) endozoochory, diaspores inside the animal;

b) synzoochory, diaspores intentionally carried, mostly in the mouth
(stomatochory) as in some birds and all ants;

c) epizoochory (formerly indicated as exozoochory), diaspores acciden-
tally carried on the outside.

Since epizoochory on various animals is not very different in character
and since this partition splits off a group with typical characters, we shall
treat this horizontal grouping separately, after the classes created according
to agents. This inconsistency (not maintained everywhere) may be forgiven
because it yields practical results.

E. Birds and Ornithochory

The following subclasses can be distinguished;

1. Epizoochores

2. Synzoochores ——————— ⌈———— stomatochores
                          ⌊———— dyszoochores

3. Endozoochores ——————— ⌈———— accidental
                          ⌊———— adapted ——————— ⌈———— edible diaspores
                                                ⌊———— mimesis

1. Epizoochory by Birds

There are two reasons for dealing with this group separately here, even though birds rarely transport burr-like diaspores, as observations show and as their preening habits suggest. Moreover, birds living high up in trees have little chance of meeting spiny diaspores. In the tropics there exists one notorious genus of trees, *Pisonia* (Nyctaginaceae) with very sticky fruits. Large birds in both hemispheres can be covered by them and severely hampered in their movements, while small ones can be immobilized to death. *Cordia* fruits can join in. There is proof that distant islands can be colonized in this way by viscid and barbed diaspores with the aid of large sea birds (cf. *Remusatia* on p. 12 and the subchapter on island floras). Many species of *Pisonia* are found on Pacific Islands, burrs of *Acaena* were found on migrating petrels arriving in oceanic islands.

The most frequent method, however, is by means of small, unadapted diaspores present in the mud sticking to the feet of waterfowl. DARWIN already investigated this, collecting and sowing the diaspores. RIDLEY devoted seven pages to examples — species of *Juncus, Carex, Polygonum, Glyceria, Cyperus, Alisma, Hottonia,* etc., describing cases of the sudden appearance of such plant species along the margins of isolated ponds. On p. 549 he gives an enumeration of small-seeded plants possibly brought to islands in this way.

2. Synzoochorous Bird Diaspores

First we present the case of the edible diaspores of *Viscum album* carried in the beak, in which the viscid seed is reported to be immediately redeposited when the bird whets its bill on branches. This was said to be done regularly by mistle-thrushes *(Turdus viscivorus)* spezialized to some degree on the fruits; however, most of the seeds are just regurgitated from the gizzard or pass completely through the animal (endozoochory). The viscid part of the endocarp makes for ideal dispersal, viz. to the righ substrate, with establishment ensured. In most instances the pericarp is eaten as a whole. In North-America species of *Phoradendron* are dispersed by various birds (McATEE, 1947).

The tropical family of flower-peckers (Dicaeidae) is specialized on Loranthaceae in a double respect. Its representatives take nectar from the flowers and have a gizzard with a special structure, allowing the seeds to pass through, whereas insects are retained. The rind only is rejected from the bill. Long strings of excreted seeds infect trees (see Fig. 6). DOCTERS VAN LEEUWEN (1954) wrote an extensive monograph for Java. Other birds participate.

Many birds are alleged to act as dyszoochores (MÜLLER-SCHNEIDER, 1933) when they eat diaspores and digest them. Thus, wood-pigeons are reported as dystrophic to *Fagus* and *Quercus*, but they may disgorge or drop some of the "nuts".

Thrushes, waxwings and crows can disgorge large seeds and kernels, as tucans do with the large stones of palms *(Euterpe)*. This means transition between syn- and endozoochory.

Real synzoochory of a partly dyszoochorous character results when nut-collecting birds cache part of their food or place it somewhere to be pecked, but neglect to eat it. The survival of diaspores in this case seems entirely accidental and incidental, but when this happens regularly to even a small percentage the method can be regarded as the normal dispersal mechanism for many plant species, just as wind-dispersal, which also involves great losses, is the normal mechanism for pollen of wind-pollinated flowers. For seeds, the method described must have started in Gymnosperms (large *Pinus* and *Araucaria* seeds in Europe and America) (SWANBERG, 1951). *Pinus cembra* is actually spread in this way by squirrels, woodpeckers and nut-crackers in the Alps near the forest limit. Best known for this method among the animals are the nut-crackers *(Nucifraga)*, feeding largely on "nuts" *(Fagus, Quercus, Juglans, Castanea, Corylus)*. *Garrulus* species (jays), also rooks have been observed to bury hazel nuts and acorns (CHETTLEBURGH, 1952). In North-America the pigeon *Columba fasciata* (eating seeds of *Quercus, Pinus, Prunus)* and even some woodpeckers are considered as forest planters (McATEE, 1947). The California woodpecker *(Balanosphyra)* can embed thousands of acorns, almonds and pecan-nuts *(Carya)* in bark-fissures or in holes, made in the bark. This dyszoochory rarely has a dispersal-effect, but rodents may steal the embedded diaspores and store them underground. SCHUSTER (1950) gave a fine description of the activity of *Garrulus glandarius* in Germany, where on the average each bird transported 4600 acorns in one season. Many birds flew with them to a forest at 4 km distance. The average is much less, but extremes do count here. MÜLLER-SCHNEIDER (1955) gave a detailed review of these cases. I go into this matter somewhat more deeply because of the doubts of WEBB (in HAWKES, 1966). He challenges the effect of rooks carrying acorns and found no correspondence between the time (2000 years) the mixed oak forest took to spread over the British Isles (assumed to start in south-west England so that each generation of 20 years had to advance 60 miles) and the dispersal possibility, excluding man. (Migrating nut-crackers may have provided larger steps).

However, one should not be rash in blaming ecology as being "defective". The bedbug was used by WEBB as a comparison, being well known for having no wings but getting to places nonetheless. Being familiar with hygiene, one has to admit that it is possibly carried by man. The bug may also be in the premises! (This is a pun).

Aesculus hippocastanum could not follow the retiring ice in Europe and failed to regain its old territory in the North mainly for lack of finding (new) disseminators, as *Quercus* did.

Wild boars are probably purely destructive for all diaspores discussed here. In considering *Quercus* and *Castanea* and their difficult dispersal, one should not forget that the genera were originally at home in the humid tropics, where a large seed is more important than a fast seed (p. 87). A study of their dispersal there is sorely needed as we have only a few data on nibbling squirrels (RIDLEY p. 377).

In cases of biotic dispersal, the synecological aspect should be taken into account, i. e., the fact that the biotope in unconquered land should fit the dispersing animal. A jay has no natural disposition to cache acorns in a distant, open heath. As we shall see, a mixed diet of the animal and its nesting in outlying territories, also the presence of preceding trees with a mixed dispersal or with mixed attraction (*Pinus* species) can aid in accessibility of the region in regard to birds.

The historical checking of dispersal can in this book only be touched upon here and there. The subject lends itself more to writings of a geographically limited scope. For post-glacial history in Scandinavia, I mention the investigations of FIRBAS (1935) on the shifting, with time, of the distributional limits of some forest trees. For *Alnus, Betula* and *Corylus* these agree with the findings of dispersal ecology; for *Pinus sylvestris* and *Ulmus montana* they exceed regular possibilities. MÜLLER-SCHNEIDER (1955) suggested here some influence of exceptional dispersal, not of a community but of a pioneer. Incidental accessibility of the habitat and the reverse, the occurrence of barriers, play a role here, as is obvious in the Alps, where descent into valleys was easy.

3. Endozoochory

a) **Non-adapted Diaspores.** We might start with the most primitive method, the indiscriminate swallowing of diaspores together with foliage, but in this case the possibility is just theoretical.

Next comes the mainly dystrophic, dyszoochorous action of granivorous birds feeding on dry fruits and seeds. These are often shelled in the beak and ground so thoroughly in gizzard and stomach that they are destroyed. Agriculturists considered the activity as favourable for getting rid of weed seeds. Old countings of KEMPSKI for pigeons and hens gave in regard to *Lithospermum* and *Rumex* that 4 % of the seeds passed intact, of which 25 % would germinate. Recent research on the droppings of pheasants,

Fig. 2. Dehisced follicle-pod of Archidendron vaillantii. (From BAILEY-Compr. Cat. of Queensland Pl.)

crows, sparrows, wood-pigeons, and starlings showed that the percentage may be even higher. See also RIDLEY (p. 439), KREFTING and ROE (1949) and SAGAR and HARPER (1961).

Ducks swallow large quantities of seeds, a proportion of which also remains intact. RIDLEY gives six pages on different species, stressing the influence of their migrations on plant dispersal and distribution. This is most important for Cyperaceae, but also for species of *Nymphaea, Nuphar, Pontederia,* and even for some plants with berries. For *Potamogeton* see p. 100 for the clear zoochory in cyperaceous *Gahnia* see p. 38.

DEVLAMING and PROCTOR (1968) investigated experimentally and quantitatively the periods of retention and the relative viability of many aquatic diaspores inside some shore- and waterbirds. They confirmed many old positive assumptions on such dispersal, but emphasized the limitation to small and hard diaspores, apparently more or less (pre-)adapted in this respect, perhaps collateral to hydrochory (thus diplochory). This refers to some Cyperaceae and some species of *Potamogeton* and *Sagittaria,* where

Fig. 3. Dehisced fruits of Paeonia mlokosewitchi with smooth, blue, fertile and wrinkled, red, sterile seeds, both juicy. (Photo NATAN)

often dispersal over far more than one thousand miles by widely migrating waterfowl (and increased germinability) seems ensured. Such dispersal means a large loss of diaspores but this is counterbalanced by directed dispersal to favourable sites.

b) Adapted Diaspores. The bulk of the ornithochores have diaspores adapted to fruit-eating birds, that excrete the hard part undamaged.

Here too one should be reticent in relying on superficial observation of feeding. Some protein-loving birds (e. g. tits) have been reported as taking also berries and drupes, but are dyszoochorous by destroying the seeds. *Coccothraustus,* the hawfinch, got for this reason the melodious German name of "Kirschkernbeisser" (destroying cherry-stones).

Temperate regions, as a consequence of having fruitless periods, possess few birds which feed exclusively on juicy fruits. Few fruits *(Prunus, Ribes)* mature in summer there. Wood-pigeons, preferring acorns and beech-mast but accepting cereals, later switch to berries (as documented in the case of *Ilex* and *Hedera*). Thrushes switch from insects, etc. to fruits. Some of these *(Hippophae, Berberis, Rosa)* are accepted by them only late in the season, in some regions not at all, so that the fruits have to rely on wind dispersal when dry. Many *(Juniperus, Cotoneaster, Sorbus, Cornus, Ligustrum)* last through the winter locally as "Wintersteher", being consumed in a certain sequence. MÜLLER-SCHNEIDER (1955) lists a number of berries never consumed in Europe, probably because the natural specialist-birds have become rare. Much literature on bird-dispersal in North-America (94 items) has been compiled by McATEE (1947).

Pure fruit-eaters can form a permanent part of forest ecology in the tropics, as described on p. 86. Some belong to the thrushes and pigeons, having different tastes there and swallowing larger kernels than in Europe.

The paper by PHILIPPS (1926), quoted extensively by RIDLEY (p. 499), gives details on African birds. I quote many *Olea* and *Elaeocarpus* species, the seeds of which may be carried for miles by birds. In Indonesia the fruit-pigeons *(Carpophaga)* played a role in history by eating nutmeg with its arilloid (the mace) and disseminating it outside the region set aside for its culture by the East India Company, with nasty results for the innocent inhabitants. They also carry the large, greenish drupes of *Canarium* and *Elaeocarpus* spp. Actual dispersal by such fruit-eaters is limited by fast evacuation (sometimes after one half-hour), but may have played a role in some Pacific Islands as shown by the case of *Myristica.* Many showy arilloid seeds are present in the tropics, even among Euphorbiaceae, as shown in the chapter on arilloids. Seeds even larger than those of *Myristica* are devoured by cassowaries. Other important tropical fruit-eaters are the barbets (Capitonidae), tucans and hornbills (Bucerotidae). The latter also swallow large diaspores, such as those of *Areca* palms and the arillode-seeds of *Afzelia* (see Fig. 10).

c) The Syndrome of Bird-diaspores. Birds have only a weak sense of smell, or none at all, and are purely visual animals. In recent experiments on pigeons with amylacetate the lowest concentration producing "olfactory" reaction was double that allowed in factories to avoid irritation of eyes and

throat. Birds can climb and fly but have no teeth. The botanical answer is
that diaspores have:

1. an attractive edible part;
2. an outer protection against premature eating (green/acid);
3. an inner protection of the seed against digestion; (kernel, bitter or
   with toxic substances)
4. signaling colours when mature;
5. no smell (although smell is no impediment when present);
6. permanent attachment;
7. no special place for the whole;
8. no closed, hard rind;
9. in hard fruits the seeds exposed or dangling.

Just as in the pollination classes of flowers, each individual feature can
be lacking. Specialized birds are perfectly capable of finding greenish fruits,
but the ideal case is a brilliant diaspore, with contrasting colours, preferably
assisted by coloured auxiliary organs. *Sterculia* fruits look like two-coloured
flowers. In *Ochna* the torus, in many *Clerodendron* species the calyx provides contrasting colours, as do the red arils on black seeds. In the simplest
cases, as in *Magnolia,* only the coloured sarcotesta seeds are showy. Additional edible parts are numerous, as will become clear in the chapter on arilloids.
In the giant cactus *(Carnegiea)* birds eat the seeds with the surrounding pulp.
In many cacti this consists of juicy, swollen funicles, wound around the
seed, and exposed by dehiscence of the fleshy pericarp. Just as in bird-
flowers, red dominates. We are not sure whether this is based on innate
preference of birds, better perception, better contrast with the foliage, or on
the colour combination being a signal learned by association. The second
best combination is dark blue with a ligther hue. For two colours see Fig. 3.

The dimensions are usually smaller than in fruits for mammals (which
possess teeth), but sometimes large fruits can be pecked into fragments or
they split open in spite of their fleshiness; some species of *Momordica,
Gardenia, Fagraea, Cereus,* Lardizabalaceae. In the genus *Ficus* small,
coloured, axillary figs are eaten by birds. The presentation of the diaspores
proper on hanging funicles (or improvised organs) can be observed in species
of *Acacia* (see Fig. 4, 5), *Magnolia, Xylopia, Eremurus, Anthurium, Gahnia,
Euonymus, Xanthoxylum.* In other cases *(Archidendron)* (see Fig. 2) torsion of the valves provides exposition.

Citrus fruits (hesperidia) deviate from the ornithochorous type by
possessing an indehiscent, repellent and tough pericarp and by the large
seeds, separating easily from the sweet pulp when pecked at. I found no
data on dispersal in their natural environment. RIDLEY, however, cited data
from Jamaica, where an *Icterus* and a turtledove feed on the fruits and
cause spontaneous growth of seedlings. The type fits better to monkeys. In

N. Australia cockatoos destroy *Citrus* fruits for the sake of the seeds. Some seeds may escape destruction after transport.

Temperate weeds are as a rule not ornithochorous, but there exist some weed-like shrubs and trees that spread rapidly through regions by means of birds. Bews (1917) described for South-Africa the role of birds as almost the only agents of dispersal in the succession in the "thornveld", in the phase after the grasses and before the establishment of trees (see p. 42). In this inter-mediate phase almost no further anemochores appeared.

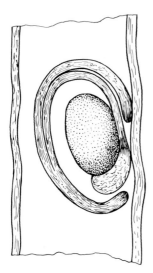

For the succession on the island of Krakatau see p. 89, for new polders see p. 91. In Europe, *Prunus serotina* has become a nuisance in woods. In Java, *Lantana* conquered open country in a few years, in New Zealand and Brazil species of *Rubus* did the same.

Fig. 4. Seed of Acacia falcata encircled by juicy, folded funicle

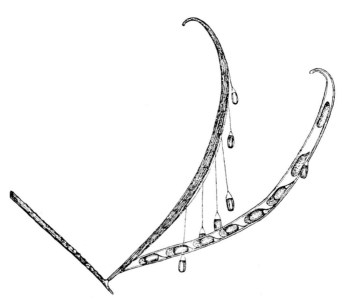

Fig. 5. Acacia australis. Woody pod dehisced, seeds on thread-like funicles with swollen tips (After Velenovsky)

d) Oil-containing Fruits. We already quoted a certain range of preference according to the taste of birds. This is obvious in the case of oily pericarps. The olive is eaten by crows and magpies, not true vegetarians. Likewise, fruits of wild *Olea* species in Africa are consumed by pigeons, but also by diverse mammals such as dogs and wild cats, so the oil can be said to bring the fruits into the range of carnivores, as we shall also see in mammal-fruits *(Persea)*. The same applies to the Oil Palm *(Elaeis)*, which has a special oil-squirrel *(Protoxerus)* of unknown dispersal effect; it is effectively dispersed by vultures. One of these *(Gyphohierax angolensis)* has such a preference for the fruits that in West Africa it is referred to as the palm-nut vulture. Even in an oil-palm plantation in Surinam a local vulture *(Coragyps atratus)* switched to the fruits. The famous oil-bird *(Steatornis)* in Central America also preferentially collects oil-fruits in its gizzard, some from palms *(Euterpe* and *Martinezia* species, *Jessenia oligocarpo)*, some from *Lonchocarpus* and *Protium* species. Like bats, it feeds on the wing at night. The possibility of convergence with bat-fruits should be studied.

Fig. 6. Kernels of Loranthaceae excreted on a branch by a bird (Dicaeum), germinating and connected by viscin. Large ones of Macrosolen cochinsinensis, small ones of Viscum articulatum (hyperparasite). (After Docters van Leeuwen)

e) Remarks on Evolution. We have seen, and shall later document this in detail, that ornithochory is normal in primitive Magnoliaceae and Leguminosae with sarcotesta and arilloids. In higher families with wind dispersal certain genera switched back to animals *(Vanilla* in the Orchidaceae, *Melocanna* in the Gramineae). In the Compositae, endozoochorous ornithochory developed terminally in a few genera with a fleshy pericarp *(Wulfia, Clibadium)*; in Labiatae, this happened in the Prasieae. We shall see later how profoundly the calyx of Labiatae is sometimes transformed for dispersal, often included in the functional fruit. It is, therefore, no wonder that in the genus *Hoslundia* the calyx has become fleshy.

I am not informed on the geological time of emergence of fruit-birds, but the change from reptiles must have been easy. Sinnott and Bailey

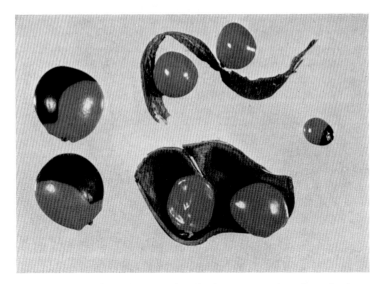

Fig. 7. Some mimetic leguminous seeds, of Abrus precatorius, Ormosia dasycarpa (both twocoloured), Adenanthera pavonina and an other species of Ormosia. (Photo NATAN)

Fig. 8. Dehisced pods of Rhynchosia mannii (from a herbarium specimen) showing persisting, red corolla and mimetic seeds. (Photo NATAN)

Fig. 9. Dehisced fruits of Allium tricoccum with mimetic seeds. (Photo NATAN)

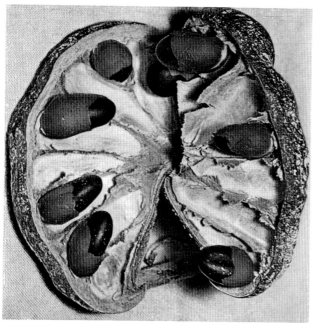

Fig. 10. Afzelia africana. Dehisced woody pod. Seeds black with red arilloid.
(After DE WIT)

(1915) connected a change in fruit types with the change from the arborescent habit to the herbaceous habit of modern times in temperate regions. Birds there are said to be reluctant to feed on the ground, so that ornithochory diminished in favour of other mechanisms. I have objections, but they are not those of BANCROFT (1930), who claimed that dry fruits are frequent among amentiferous trees, which he considered to be primitive plants. In Leguminosae the later switch to anemochory also occurred in high trees, as exemplified by Piptadenieae (see p. 124).

Fig. 11. Adenanthera pavonina. Dehisced and twisted pod with attached, mimetic seeds

We saw before that, as in the field of pollination, connections in dispersal often repose on utilization of cross-links in a pre-existing ecosystem, not on concurrent evolution of the plant and animal species under consideration, and neither on some plan behind both. This will become especially clear in the following paragraph, where the natural link reposes on deceit (cf. deceit in flower-pollination).

f) **Mimesis (imitative seeds).** This part of endozoochory has such special features that I shall deal with it as a separate topic.

In entomology, the term mimesis or mimicry refers to imitative colouring of edible animals (usually insects) to avoid being eaten by predators (often birds). A distasteful animal serves as the model. In the botanical literature, imitative colouring of seeds is seen as functional to obtain the reverse effect; edibility is suggested. In seeds, the term mimesis often refers to black and contrasting red colouring, a scheme also found frequently among the "warning colouring" of insects; however, the birds concerned with seeds are not pure insectivores and are therefore not repelled by this combination.

Certain tropical fruits produce seeds that resemble primarily the berry-like ornithochorous seeds of *Magnolia* and *Archidendron* described on p. 123 and consequently also berries in general. The seeds can deceive the visual birds. Feeding experiments by the writer in Java with the mimetic seeds of *Adenanthera pavonina* proved that granivorous birds refused them, whereas fructivorous birds (barbets) accepted them as berries, defecating them intact. Cockatoos tried to crack the very smooth, hard and slippery seeds of *Abrus* with the tip of their bills but had no success and tried several seeds in succession so that at last quite a number collected in the rear of the beak. Very young and wrinkled seeds were easier to destroy.

The deceit can, of course, only work in nature as long as its practitioners form a minority amidst really nourishing models. The same (in the opposite direction) goes for mimicry in insects.

I do not know if the passing through birds promotes germination here. In untreated seeds of *Adenanthera*, the latter process may take a year. The very hard palissade testa also fits them for life outside the rain forest. Many taxa with hard, mimetic seeds live in steppe regions. GUPPY (1912) criticized here "facile acceptance of adaptation", considering the event as just a utilization, as not more than the exhibition of seeds by a decaying orange. I leave it at that. The visual attraction of birds by accessory devices is present. The ancestral torsion of valves is maintained for exhibition purposes. It is obvious in *Adenanthera pavonina* where the inner sides of the valves are yellow (see Fig. 11). In some genera the gradual transformation of juicy sarcotesta seeds into dry mimetic seeds is based on diminishing thickness of the testa *(Paeonia)*. Another case, already cited by CORNER (1953), is *Guarea* in the Meliaceae.

I have as yet been unable to ascertain the occurrence of the type in Euphorbiaceae, but it may occur in the genera *Glochidion* and *Macaranga*, where beside species with a coloured sarcotesta some are mentioned as having dry, glistening, exposed seeds. A case in point may be a *Phyllanthus (Cicca, Prosorus)* species, e. g., *Ph. nobilis* (S. America) with beautiful, blue seeds or kernels. CARLQUIST (1966) suggested deceit for some Hawaiian Rutaceae such as *Pelea*. Perhaps *Musa calosperma* (New Guinea) is a case.

Another case is found in the Liliaceae, viz. *Allium tricoccum* (Fig. 9) from North America. This species stands beside others where the testa is soft and eaten by ants, or still others where the arilloids act as elaiosomes. *Allium tricoccum* differs by having permanently attached, erect, globular, large and glistening black, but hard seeds. An investigation of the stomach contents of local birds should confirm the suspicion of deceit. The woody biotope where I found the species is rich in real berries near the ground.

The type abounds in Leguminosae. In the Mimosoideae, e. g., *Adenanthera* and species of *Pithecellobium;* in the Caesalpinioideae, *Batesia floribunda,* perhaps *Cassia costata;* in the Papilionideae, species of *Abrus, Ormosia, Rhynchosia* and *Erythrina*. Obviously impressed by the likeness, RIDLEY called the condition an imitation-aril. In *Pithecellobium* s. l., some species concerned are *P. clypearia* and *P. lusorium*. The Australian species *P. hendersonii* is certainly ornithochorous, probably deceptive. See Fig. 7.

The genus *Erythrina* has many species with "coral seeds". In the steppe genus *Rhynchosia,* all seeds have the hard palisade testa typical for the subfamily, but remnants of some arilloid are present. The two-seeded pods are rarely indehiscent (then adhesive). In many dehiscent pods the torsion of the valves is weak and their seeds are rather flat, smooth and brown, marbled with black. In the section *Phaseoloides* we meet mimetic bluish-black seeds, sometimes (in *Rh. phaseoloides* and the probably conspecific *Rh. pyramidalis* in S. America) conspicuously red and black. They resemble those of *Abrus precatorius* but with reversion of the colour distribution, viz. with the red part near the hilum. The section *Cyanospermum* has a further refinement for ornithochory, viz. the persistence and possibly even postfloral enlargement of the corolla or at least parts thereof (the standard). In the dry petals the red colour becomes even more pronounced than it is during anthesis, when the red is present only in the standard or as stripes on a yellow background. BUCHWALD (1895) already pointed to the gaudiness of the pods, that look like three-coloured flowers in the African species *Rh. tomentosa, Rh. cyanospermum* and *Rh. calycina*. I was able to investigate in greater detail *Rh. mannii* (see Fig. 8) and *Rh. pycnostachya,* where the torsion of the valves is so pronounced that the globular blue seeds are turned outwards in prominent fashion, one by each valve, so that they contrast with the peculiar silvery, light-green tinge of the valves (here exposing their exterior sides) as well as with the stone-red, dry corolla. The seeds are dark brown but with a superficial blue sheen that gives a watery impression. The persistence of the corolla is not strictly confined to ornithochorous species but seems to be exploited there more specifically. I found this condition also (although the corolla is less obvious in this case) in a strophiolate species, *Rh. acuminatissima,* which has been placed in a different section (see p. 125).

Some Cyperaceae show botanical mimesis *de novo,* not on a sarcotesta basis. It concerns, moreover, fruits or even fruits surrounded by an extra bract. The tropical and less aquatic genus *Gahnia* relies on "intentional" consumption by birds other than ducks as its fruitlets are conspicuous by their colour and by an exposed, often dangling, position outside the dark fruiting complexes. BENL (1937) described how the loosened fruitlets are kept attached to the outside in four different ways, demonstrating the ecological importance of this condition. Often the fruitlets are glistening red, orange or yellow. I include them here under mimesis because the very hard envelope must prevent digestion of the inner parts, because the fruits do attract fructivorous birds, and because *G. mannii* even has the typical red plus black coloration. The only instance of *Gahnia* fruits found inside a bird (see RIDLEY and BENL) refers to *Pycnonotus bimaculatus,* a mainly frugivorous bulbul feeding on berries in Javanese mountains. The fruits were found in the stomach together with seeds of a *Vaccinium.* The bird also collects the small drupes of *Myrica javanica* (4 mm), and probably the sympatric fleshy, red pseudocarps of *Carex baccans* with which type *Gahnia* fruits may be confused. The originally reduced fruits of such Cyperaceae repeat secondarily (just as those of the *Siparuna* discussed on p. 114) diverse adaptations of real seeds, including arils. Aril imitation can be observed in the genus *Scleria* and relatives (see Pl. XV in RIDLEY, who mentions the fruits of a *Scleria* as being found inside birds).

F. Mammals as Dispersers

1. General

The Europe-centered literature has not produced a generally accepted special term for dispersal by mammals, a phenomenon better developed or preserved in tropical regions. The diaspores show essentially the same characteristics as those connected naturally with birds and the two phenomena of bird- and mammal-mediated dispersal show a parallel differentiation in methods. Many fruits are eaten by both birds and mammals.

The above-mentioned differentiation shows a larger share of epi (exo) -zoochores, treated separately in sub-chapter K. This is connected with the rougher fur of mammals and their life on the ground. The differentiation in the structure of the endozoochorous diaspores is more pronounced, in agreement with the strong diversity in mammals.

2. Dyszoochory and Rodents

Dyszoochory is frequent when animals digest the diaspores. Rodents like squirrels, rats and hamsters destroy those of oaks, pines and cereals. They are considered as especially harmful in American desert-like regions, although after rains seeds always germinate, having apparently escaped the onslaught in great number. Especially burrowing rodents may, however, (like the *Spalax* described before) dig up underground diaspores and all may abandon or cache them underground. This is comparable to the syn-zoochory described for nut-collecting birds. The kangaroo-rats *(Dipodomys)* in America store desert seeds. When doing this with *Prosopis* they contribute

to reforestation, or (from the viewpoint of grazing for cattle) to deteriora-
tion. I have to quote repeatedly RIDLEY's observations on squirrels on
Quercus and *Castanea* in tropical Asia, where the cups help in transport
and the spines on the cupules cause the squirrels to transport the entire
spikes to a quiet spot where parts are dropped. I also refer to his data
(p. 380) on American squirrels storing large, wingless seeds of *Pinus* and
thus acting as planters in the neighbourhood. He may be right in assuming
that the hard, waxy arilloids of the leguminous plant *Sindora* and of *Neesia*
are especially attractive to rodents. Tropical porcupines may be purely
destructive, but tropical squirrels are (like tropical pigeons) more specifically fruit-eaters, digesting only the fleshy parts. They disperse the hard
drupes of *Canarium*, *Elaeocarpus* and the like over a small distance in the
forest. This also holds true for *Theobroma cacao*, where rodents eat only
the sarcotesta-pulp around the seeds, and for the sarcotesta seeds of some
species of *Nephelium*, *Baccaurea*, and *Calamus*, where the fruits possess
hard skins and lack the smell of typical mammal-fruits. SERNANDER (1927)
called this way of dispersal glirochory (glires = rodents).

BURKART (1939, 1943) quoted data on the chinchilla, which can only
exist in the wild where *Balsamodendron brevifolium* (Leguminosae) grows.
It stores and eats the fruits (algarobillas). The important contribution of
HUBER (1910) contains the solution of the riddle as to how *Bertholletia
excelsa*, the Brazil nut, is dispersed and regenerates in nature. Its woody
capsules with internal, arilloid pulp around the seeds can be opened by man
only with the aid of an axe. Large rodents (agoutis, *Dasyprocta*) can open
them and bury the seeds as a reserve. Some *Lecythis* species have the same
bond with these animals.

3. Accidental Endozoochory

Browsing animals can swallow diaspores together with the foliage and
partly evacuate them intact. In ruminants, this dispersal can hardly be
separated from directed, intentional gathering of adapted diaspores. Many
investigations concerned the diaspores in the dung of vegetarian mammals,
including hares. They were often carried out to explain the mass-infestation
with weeds after dunging. Amaranthaceae, Chenopodiaceae, *Ranunculus*,
Urtica, many grasses, and also leguminous herbs (like *Trifolium* species)
with small pods and hard seeds, can withstand digestion to some extent.
For percentages of survival I refer to RIDLEY (p. 336—341) and the tables
in MÜLLER-SCHNEIDER (1955, p. 88—92). This is not the occasion to discuss
in detail the agricultural effect, but one archaeological effect may be mentioned. Seeds of *Chenopodium album* were found in prehistoric dwellings
in such masses that some investigators considered it to be an ancient food
plant. MÜLLER-SCHNEIDER (1959) made it clear that the layers found
consisted of animal dung.

We also pass over here the effect which passing through animals has on germination; later on, we shall see that seedling development is often accelerated. Many agriculturalists prefer such "animal-treated" seed for sowing. In South Africa, eating of leguminous pods by antelopes was seen to produce not only faster germination but also to prevent attack by insects which damage uneaten seeds for the larger part.

4. Adaptive Endozoochory

Mimetic deceit (which, in the case of mammals, would have to be by means of smell) cannot be expected. The rest of the chapter can, therefore, be devoted to intentional intake of diaspores by various mammals, all with different ethology. The general syndrome of diaspores adapted to dispersal by mammals has much in common with the one of ornithochores, mentioned before. In some points it deviates, according to the different ethology and sense-physiology of the agents. Mammals have teeth, masticate much better, are mostly larger, rarely lead an arboreal life, and are mostly night-feeders that are colour-blind. The corresponding differential characteristics of dia-spores eaten by mammals are: possession of a hard skin which offers no impediment; a more-evident protection of the seed proper against mechanical destruction, the protection often being assisted or replaced by the presence in the seed of toxic or bitter substances; a smell favourable for attraction; non-essentiality of colour; large size in a number of cases. Just as in earlier reptile-fruits, the demands of accessibility are more stringent than in bird-fruits, and dropping may be continued. For a good relation with flying mammals (bats), special requirements are evident as will be shown later. This syndrome represents again a maximum. It is, just as in ecological flower classes, partly positive (attracting legitimate visitors) and partly negative (excluding others).

In Northern regions so few original mammalian dispersers survive and so many edible fruits are introductions, that it is difficult to reconstruct original relations. The influence of ungulates on fruits remained small after glaciation when grass was present in sufficient quantities. In fruitless periods, migration or a switch in menu was not as easy as it was in birds. Fruit-bats stayed away entirely after glaciation, as did flower-birds. Some rodents could survive in the habitat or reconquer it by storing dry diaspores of the advancing plants. The natural role of martens, jackals, and hedgehogs has largely to be surmised. Wild boars represent the villains of the piece, although in South America the peccary is beneficial to the low-growing, fragrant ananas. We have to speculate on the inclusion in our classification system, as mammal-fruits, of the following items: medlars *(Mespilus)*, melons, peaches, apples, pears, prunes, cucumbers, etc. — fruits which have, moreover, been grossly modified by cultivation. The sweet-smelling green quince *(Cydonia)* is a typical mammal-fruit. Bears had and have a modest role as eaters of berries, also as consumers of larger fruits. The tropics offer a rich and permanent table for fructivores such as monkeys, civet-cats, bats, ungulates, bears, etc. The fruits and the animals reflect each other's characteristics there. In contrast to other handbooks (Europe-centered), the one by ULBRICH (1928) tries to bring this out for tropical fruits.

Ungulates. Tropical ruminants and elephants eat all kinds of vegetable matter that agree with their taste. Elephants mix fruit in their herbage and in Africa even follow the fruiting of preferred trees, e. g. of *Dumoria heckeli*, with large seeds. The tree is said to be distributed along the trails. The very large kernels (13 cm) of the palm *Borassus flabellifer* vere also found sprouting in the dung, together with those of *Hyphaene* and *Adansonia* and the many leguminous pods discussed below. For details see PHILIPPS (1926) and BURTT (1929). In Asia, *Durio* and *Mangifera* seeds were found sprouting in the dung.

Ruminants in African savanna-regions rely for a considerable part on fruits. Antelopes can digest rather woody fruits such as those of *Adansonia*. Many Leguminosae, especially *Acacia* species, specialize in this way of dispersal, offering leathery, nutritive pods, sometimes keeping them on the tree, but mostly dropping them immediately at maturity. The fruits are often classified incorrectly as dry. A special adaptive point is the extreme hardness of the seeds, resistant to strong molars, as evident in *Tamarindus, Dichrostachys, Acacia,* and those *Cassia* species with hard, indehiscent pods of the type of *C. fistula. Acacia arabica* and *A. horrida* are mentioned as pioneers in grassland, spread by ruminants (also goats). Some of those trees, including species of *Prosopis, Ceratonia,* and *Samanea,* are even cultivated in diverse parts of the world, also in South America, as cattle fodder under the general name of algarobba (properly *Ceratonia*). In North America, *Lespedeza stricta* (Papilionaceae) was spread by cattle in this way.

Bats and Chiropterochory. The writer has published a monograph on the subject (1957 b), of which the following is an abstract. In tropical Asia and Africa, the old group of Macrochiroptera (fundamentally fruit-eaters) has a large influence. In America, fruit-eaters developed later independently and incompletely among Microchiroptera in some of the Phyllostomidae: viz. separately in the sub-families Stenoderminae, Phyllonycterinae, and Glossophaginae.

As experience with expatriate fruits teaches, attractiveness of bat-fruits is international, obviously depending on some general preference in bats. The taste and consistency can vary between hard-sour and soft-sweet, but otherwise a syndrome of general characteristics can easily be recognized, in accordance with the ethology and sense-physiology of the bats. Fruit-bats are nocturnal and colour blind, have a keen sense of smell, and have, apparently, an innate preference for "stale", musty odours like the one their own glands produce. Rarely (in the case of small-seeded *Ficus* and *Piper* species) do they ingest seeds or kernels, mostly consuming just the juice after intense chewing. After transport to a suitable place, the remnants are regurgitated, sometimes at the roosting places. The distance is not large, rarely surpassing 200 m. The larger species *(Pteropus)* can transport heavy mangoes, but other species have lower limits for loads. Fruit-bats have above all, difficulty in flying through dense foliage as their sonar-apparatus is weakly developed.

The fruit-syndrome is, accordingly: drab colour, musty odour reminding one of fermentation and rancid substances (butyric acid), possibly large size with possession of large seeds, permanent attachment with exposure outside the foliage. The latter position can (as in bat-flowers, described in FAEGRI and VAN DER PIJL, 1966) be realized by a curious reorganization of the tree-structure, resulting in (e. g.) an open structure of the canopy (pagoda-structure, as in *Terminalia catappa*), projecting stalks, long stalks hanging underneath the canopy (flagellicarpy), or placement on the main trunk (caulicarpy as in species of *Lansium*, *Ficus*, and *Artocarpus*). The occurrence of fleshy fruits with a caulicarpous position has struck many early observers in the tropics. This was explained by them in many ways, none of which can be accepted, but the connection with bats for either pollination or dispersal is a satisfactory explanation. Entire reorganization of the crown of the female trees is conspicuous in the bat-dispersed species *Chlorophora excelsa* (Moraceae), as described by EGGELING (1955) and OSMASTON (1965). A possible relation between darkness and odour production should be studied.

A long list of cases can be found in my paper (1957), also a few in KUHLMANN (1947). Some cases deserve comment here, firstly from the viewpoint of human consumption. In contrast to temperate table-fruits, those in the tropics rarely *(Capsicum)* represent gaudy ornithochores, being instead mostly large and drab with a smell to which one has to become accustomed. Instances are species of *Artocarpus*, *Achras*, *Psidium* and wild types of *Mangifera*.

Another link with man is that "ghost-trees" in international folklore are visited at night by crying bats; their visits serve either pollination or seed dispersal.

The families most popular with the bats are: Palmae (including the date-palm) in which caulicarpy is organizational, Moraceae (including *Antiaris toxicaria* and many *Ficus* species), Chrysobalanaceae, Annonaceae, Sapotaceae, Anacardiaceae. The first indication was given by HUBER (1910). The few caulicarpous Leguminosae (a. o. species of *Cordyla*, *Cynometra*, *Detarium*, *Inocarpus*, and *Angylocalyx*) are mostly chiropterochorous. *Andira inermis* is even called "morceguiera" in Brazil and "andira" is an Indian native name for bat. The sole caulicarpous plant of temperate Europe *(Ceratonia)* is natural on the northern limit of African fruit-bats; its fruits, containing butyric acid, are eaten by them in time of need. In case of need, bats switch to leaves and to bird-fruits.

With regard to the evolutionary development among the flowering plants, the following can be stated: bat-fruits appear already in some Ranales, are dominant in caulicarpous and flagellicarpous *Ficus* species (including the sycamore near the northern limit of fruit-bats), but also occur in advanced groups on one level with and alternating with ornithochorous and other fruits. In the Bignoniaceae, bat-flowers seem primary, probably inducing (by the development of special odoriferous substances) the incidental switch to bat-fruits. The reverse may have happened elsewhere.

Fig. 12. Mango-fruits (Mangifera indica) dangling by weight underneath the foliage

We can also review the evolution with regard to complexity of diaspores. Bat-dispersal of nude seeds has been found in the gymnosperm *Cycas rumphii*, where it is not typical and is thus possibly a regressive overlapping. In *Cephalotaxus* the aromatic, pineapple-like fragrance of the seed may also indicate reptile-connections, especially in those cases where it is dropped. In the leguminous plant *Swartzia prouacensis,* the seed itself, still in the arilloid phase of exposed seeds, developed a bond with bats, whereas other species employing the same device are ornithochorous. Its chiropterochorous adaptations consist of a fairly large seed, a drab-white arilloid, a brown pod and a most curious funicle of up to 3 m length, so that we may speak of flagellispermy (see Fig. 13). The smell and the occurrence of bat-visits deserve investigation in Guyana. The same applies to the long-funicled seeds of *Lecythis usitata* that are, indeed, collected by bats. For the arillate but short-funicled *Lecythis zabucajo* (sapucaya-nut), the picking out of the

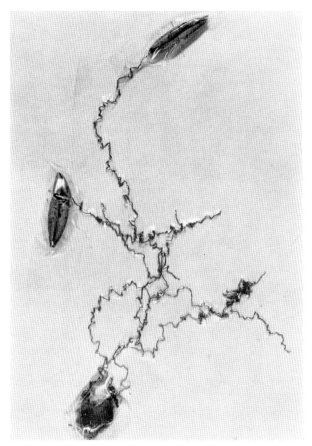

Fig. 13. Swartzia prouacensis. Dehisced valves of pod with seed taken out, the funicle still showing its folded condition inside the pod. Herbarium-specimen sticked on with tape. (Photo NATAN)

seeds from the hard fruit-boxes and their dispersal by bats already have been described by GREENHALL (1965). He records that the odour of the arilloid suggests that its tissue is rotting. Some *Inga* species will probably have to be included, standing at the point of divergence from reptiles to-wards birds and bats. Closed sarcotesta-fruits *(Lansium, Baccaurea)* are as frequent in the list as higher pericarp-fruits.

Regarding plant geography, I pointed (1957 b) to the concurrence of the limits of certain plants (such as *Spondias dulcis*) with those of fruit-bats in the Pacific, reflecting, perhaps, ancient land connections as only *Pteropus*, the flying fox, can fly tens of kilometers. Bats contributed, however, to the re-colonization of Krakatau (DOCTERS VAN LEEUWEN, 1936). In Australia, *Pteropus* has recently spread southwards, outside the tropics, following fruit cultivation but switching to new, unadapted species of plants.

It is synecologically important that some fruit-bats, especially in Africa, migrate to neighbouring regions with a different crop. A number of more or less simultaneously fruiting species can therefore form one food-association, as well as a number of subsequently fruiting species in one and the same community where bats can have a permanent base. The latter situation has been shown to exist also for flower-bats (FAEGRI and VAN DER PIJL, 1966).

Some plant species are bound to bats in a double sense, for pollination and dispersal, e. g. the wild bananas and *Sonneratia alba*. The hanging position is favourable to both processes. SIMMONDS (1959) reported that dense stands of *Musa* seedlings may be the results of the presence of a bat-colony in a tree.

Primates. Monkeys and apes are latecomers, taking advantage of ecological opportunities that open up incidentally, and forming incidental connections. They are mostly destructive, eating everything edible, ripe or unripe, also buds and leaves, soft- or hard-skinned fruits; they may or may not be instrumental in dispersal. They are not colour-blind and rely more on visual perception than other mammals do. Some externally hard fruits with internal, soft arilloids suit them better than they do birds. The wild mangosteens *(Garcinia)*, possessing such a structure, are indeed eaten by monkeys. In a cultivated form, they are eaten by man as the monkey's successor in invading the environment. Because of the absence of a bat-smell, they are even popular with newly arrived Europeans. *Mammea* is somewhat of an American counterpart. Many fruits of Euphorbiaceae, Sapindaceae, Rubiaceae *(Gardenia)*, Loganiaceae *(Strychnos)*, Sterculiaceae *(Theobroma)*, and Rutaceae *(Citrus)* are of this type.

The most curious fruit of this ecological group (armoured fruits) is the large, spiny durian *(Durio zibethinus)*. Its internal arilloid is preferred above everything else in Indonesia by orang-utans, rhinos, tapirs, bears, elephants and man as successors to reptiles (see p. 23). The opening of fallen fruits requires skill and force. The smell is overwhelming, but not of the bat-type. Mechanically, the seeds are unprotected, but on the other hand they are toxic when raw. Even elephants defecate them undamaged. The arillode contains oil so that even panthers join in the battle for the fruit. Smaller-fruited sister species are ornithochorous (with dehiscing and coloured fruit), demonstrating the divergence from the reptile-phase.

Various Mammals. STOPP (1958 b) discussed the geocarpy of *Cucumis humifructus*, apparently concurring with other cases of geocarpy in desert-like regions in Africa. The position has, however, not the character of atelochory as in those other cases (see p. 80), and the fruit is large and juicy. STOPP doubted the dispersal by aardvarks *(Orycteropus)*, near whose tunnels the plants are found. MEEUSE (1958) brought good arguments in support of the idea that the animal eats the fruit for its water and buries its dung with the seeds near its nest. Otherwise the seeds germinate badly.

The role of tapirs in Amazonia is reflected in the works of HUBER (1910) and KUHLMANN (1947). To mention a curious case reported, they bury seeds of *Araucaria angustifolia,* so that thickets of it arise on the spot.

Civet-cats *(Paradoxurus)* in Indonesia consume all kinds of fruit. They have the pleasant habit of defecating on fixed open spots, so that I could review the complete yearly menu. The data are lost, but the curious impression remains that such a small animal is able to eat the large palm-fruits of *Arenga saccharifera* and defecate the large kernels. The animals can climb trees. BARTELS (1964) published a list of seeds dispersed by *Paradoxurus hermaphroditus* in Java.

I pointed out for *Durio* that large carnivores consider its oily fruit just as attractive as herbivores do (compare carnivorous birds and the fruits of the oilpalm, *Elaeis*). Another oily fruit, the avocado *(Persea gratissima),* is sought after by wild cats and jaguars in America after being dropped. The seeds are too large to pass through birds.

We badly need information on the relations between diaspores and kangaroos in Australia. The absence of ruminants may give an interesting background to the form of *Acacia* fruits there, as it does to the relative scarceness of spines on this continent.

G. Ants and Myrmecochory

Ants are latecomers in history, so that they do not play a fundamental role; the adaptations to them in diaspores have been built on top of, and utilize, older structures. SERNANDER (1906) and BERG (1954) proved that their temperate cases were of pre-glacial origin, but pointed also to the importance of ant-dispersal for late speciation. On the other hand, ants evoke to an amazing degree responses and reorganizations in diaspores, often with such a strong and fast transference of function that closely related species use different organs for attracting ants.

An old objection to the concept that selective forces in the environment are creative, is that ecological selection follows physiological causation. One might first ask whether the origin of a mutation is physiological causation and further what induced, physiological modification can offer to selection.

The older literature has been covered in a review by UPHOFF (1942). This shows the paucity of relations between plant diaspores and the (much older) termites, which are obviously purely destructive.

One group of ants, composed of the Mediterranean and North-American harvester ants *(Messor, Atta, Tetramorium,* and *Pheidole)* is also dyszoo-chorous. They carry the most varied materials to the nest, sort them out, store the edible parts and consume these after fermentation. The dispersal-effect is small. Experiments with truly myrmecochorous seeds are necessary to study their resistance. Few are found in the "granaries".

Among dispersing vegetarian ants diverse genera collect only specialized diaspores, eating the (always white) edible part, the so-called elaiosome. This soft part got its name because it usually contains drops of an oily sub-stance — the rest of the diaspore (seed), often hard and smooth and apparently difficult to destroy, is buried in nest-tunnels or in fissures. BRESINSKY (1963) demonstrated that broadly inserted elaiosomes are separated from the seed proper by special tissues, thick-walled and con-taining crystals. One might remark that the distance is small, but more than just transport is involved, there is often also fixation in a suitable spot, thus precision dispersal. Reduc-tion in the number of seeds produced by the plant is a consequence.

Fig. 14. Diaspore of the grass Rottboelia exaltata consist-ing of two spikelets of one internodium of the spike. Elaiosome from the medulla stippled

For the root-parasites involved, such as species of *Melampyrum, Pedicularis, Mystro-petalon* and *Lathraea,* burial is important. It is curious that *Lathraea* seeds are larger and less numerous than they are in comparable parasites, such as *Orobanche.*

In simple cases, the fleshy testa itself con-tains edible material in a diffuse form. This *"Puschkinia-*type" embraces a. o. *Allium ursi-num, Tozzia alpina, Cyclamen,* and *Ornitho-galum* species. Diffuse drops of oil are present also in the seed coat of some ant-epiphytes such as *Myrmecodia,* but in some of them the connection is still more vague, as just an adhering piece of the infructescence suffices *(Procris laevigata* in Java). In most cases, a specialized elaiosome is present. My experience in Java is that the ants in question react to it like lightning, elsewhere they may act with more hesitation. At an early date, I already began to doubt that oil is the attractive factor — this on the basis of experiments with just oil. Some volatile component must be present, probably in the oil, and is rapidly perceived. The lipoid often impregnates the tender outer cell walls. BRESINSKY made it rather certain that the attractant is an unsaturated, free fatty acid, absent in nonmyrmecochorous appendages of the seed and not

always connected with visible oildrops (as in *Melica* glumes). It is probably
ricinolic acid with an oxygroup which, in pure form also, attracts ants
strongly, although its volatility is not great. It leads to the consumption of
the inner protein, lipoid, starch and vitamins (B_1 and C were found by
BRESINSKY, after WEBER and LIEB; these vitamins also occur in the ant-
bodies of myrmecotrophic plants).

SERNANDER's large monograph (1906) on European examples led to the
distinction of several types of ant-diaspores, often fruits. I shall not sum
them up, as RIDLEY and UPHOFF did, because ever more types are found in
temperate regions as well as in the tropics. Here are some more European
examples of seeds, where a caruncle is often the basis of the elaiosome:
Helleborus species, *Scilla bifolia, Galanthus nivalis, Chelidonium majus,*
and species of *Euphorbia, Stellaria, Ulex, Viola, Primula, Sarothamnus,* and
Arenaria; in *Hepatica triloba,* species of *Anemone, Ranunculus* and *Lamium,*
fruits are involved.

Most of the plants mentioned belong to the herbaceous spring flora in
northern forests. In drier Mediterranean regions, *Melica* species developed
new elaiosomes at the base of the spikelet; *Centaurea* species and other
Compositae at the base of the achene — a process accompanied by loss of
the pappus. The more tropical instances which I shall mention do not grow
in dense forest; this is true even for a few of the ant-epiphytes.

The refinement of the appeal to ants (looking for mere physiological
causation leaves us in the dark), is demonstrated by cases where an elaiosome is formed from very special organs. In *Primula acaulis* and some species
of *Melampyrum* and *Veronica,* it arises from a swelling of the funicle; in
Pedicularis sylvatica from a protruding endosperm-haustorium (BERG, 1954).
BRESINSKY described the precise ontogeny of many elaiosomes, finding in
species of *Melampyrum* and *Lathraea* that they arise from a separate part
of the endosperm. In American *Nemophila* species, the elaiosome is the
"cucullus" known for many Hydrophyllaceae. This is the outer layer of the
testa with large, living, and densely filled cells, a layer which becomes
detached and is sloughed off by the placenta. BRESINSKY diagnosed changes
in dispersal, also into myrmecochory, as important factors in speciation,
demonstrated especially for Anchuseae.

What interests us here especially is that specific modifications of the plant
as a whole occur, bringing the seeds into the life-sphere of the ants, perhaps
also protecting the tender elaiosomes against desiccation by delay in shedding. Sometimes it is rapid disintegration of the spike (in grasses), sometimes
disintegration of the fruit into irregular fragments (some Hydrophyllaceae,
some species of *Trillium, Asarum europaeum,* and *Datura fastuosa*). Often
the modification consists of early detachment of the seeds or the slackening
of non-sclerenchymatous flower (fruit) stalks, the presence of turned-down
capsules *(Cyclamen, Scoliopus),* acauly, or even reorganization of the

flowering axis, as described for species of the myrmecochore *Roscoea*. NORD-
HAGEN (1932) described this for the latter genus, a member of the Zingiberaceae from the Himalayas. Like SERNANDER, he and BERG (1958, 1959)
pointed to such changes in dispersal as influencing the plant already in or
before the flowering phase, and even as necessitating adjustment for pollination (see p. 16).

BERG (1958) studied some American examples in this respect, adding in
1966 a review of other cases of myrmecochory known there, for example,
Uvularia grandiflora, Sanguinaria canadensis, and *Asarum canadense*. In the
true pericarp-berries of liliaceous *Trillium* species, he found a retrograde
change-over to the sarcotesta as an elaiosome. They were suited to birds,
but the sustained pulpiness of the seed allowed it to form an elaiosome as
well. I refer to this, as an analogy to the forest-plants mentioned for Europe,
because the change to myrmecochory in certain species was accompanied
by a change in habitat; viz. from open field to forest. He proposed a revised
taxonomy of the genus (later also of *Scoliopus* and other relatives of *Paris*)
on the basis of dispersal-ecology. A reminder of what has been happening
elsewhere through the ages!

CROSSBY (in HAWKES, 1966) found a reproductive disadvantage in the
myrmecochorous primrose *(Primula acaulis* or *P. veris acaulis)* seeding in
woody areas. He compared it to the non-myrmecochorous, erect, cowslip
(P. veris or *P. veris officinalis* or *P. officinalis)* growing in pastures. The
precision of ant-dispersal was nullified by bad establishment of the seedlings.
We might remark that the latter factor is usually not considered under
reproductive capacity, and might also ask whether he investigated each
species in its optimal habitat, also in regard to ants. Later, BERG (1966)
added for California *Dendromecon*, the tree-poppy. This is interesting as it
concerns a tree, and a chaparral plant. Usually elaiosomes dry out quickly
in a dry atmosphere.

In the tropics scattered cases have been found, which in this textbook
will be dealt with collectively since they were often published in poorly
accessible sources (cf. v. d. PIJL, 1955 b). Berries of *Asparagus asparagoides*
are comparable to those of *Trillium*. In Malaysia, many grasses in dry
regions have a disintegrating spike with a part of the medulla adhering
to the units as a elaiosome (see *Rottboelia* in Fig. 14). Furthermore, *Loch-
nera rosea, Cleome ciliata, Sterculia alexandri, Endonema retzioides, Desmodium gyroides, Cyanastrum cardifolium, Turnera ulmifolia, Datura
fastuosa, Coluria* spp., *Mystropetalon* (a parasite infecting its host underground). In some of them parts of the placenta adhere as an elaiosome, in
Clerodendron incisum a placental part of the pericarp, usually serving for
ornithochory in the genus. *Sebastiana* in Argentine is tree-like, with the
combination of an explosive mechanism and the euphorbiaceous caruncle
as elaiosome. Some Cyclanthaceae *(Ludovia, Cyclanthus)* may be suspected

of being myrmecochorous too, and among the Papilionaceae and Euphorbiaceae there are many representatives with beetle-like seeds (e. g. *Aca-
lypha*), also in some Cactaceae *(Blassfeldia)*.

A special group of myrmecochores is formed by the ant-epiphytes of the
tropics. They live in the "ant-gardens" on trees or provide nesting places
themselves in hollows. ULE (1905) described the situation for Amazonia.

Fig. 15. Ant-garden in Java with plant and seedlings of Hoya lacunosa

Some of the Araceae and Bromeliaceae there have weakly myrmecochorous,
berry-like fruits. In Java, DOCTERS VAN LEEUWEN (1929) found true myrmecochory in those ant-epiphytes (species of *Hoya* [see Fig. 15], *Dischidia*,
Aeschynanthus), which have oil in primarily anemochorous seed-hairs; also,
there are some orchids with oil-drops in the testa. The famous "living ant-

4*

nests" of *Myrmecodia* have ant-dispersal (next to ornithochory) and offer nectar to their inhabitants. DOCTERS VAN LEEUWEN found that even some hollow-stemmed inhabited ferns had switched to myrmecochory by the formation of oil-drops in the sporangium-walls — unchanged through aeons, but now modified under the influence of ants.

When speaking about ants in general it is, even when one leaves carnivores aside, necessary to point out that finer specificity exists, especially in guests of ant-epiphytes.

H. Wind and Anemochory

1. General

It has already been mentioned (p. 19) that this way of dispersal, although perhaps numerically important, is not basic in seedplants. Its preponderance in certain regions reflects the climate and the biotic poverty and is, essentially, a feature of a pioneer vegetation. MÜLLER-SCHNEIDER (1955) cites data for the alpine flora (60 % anemochorous) and the Mediterranean garigue (50 %). For other floras, I refer to Chapter VI C.

In anemochory we can distinguish plain horizontal displacement of the air; dynamic and thermic turbulence, both culminating in cyclones; and a simple slowing down of falling diaspores by air resistance. The propelling effect of the latter on wing-like structures provides time for sideways displacement. Botanical engineers are able to work out the dynamics and the quantitative side of fall-velocity.

DINGER (1889) and SCHMIDT (1918) compared different constructions as to their possibilities and formulated technical calculations for theoretical cases. SCHMIDT calculated for many species the average limits of dispersal, the distance which 1/100 of the diaspores can reach. Assuming an average turbulence of the air of A = 20 (g. cm. sec.) and a wind velocity of 10 m/sec., he found for the spores of *Lycoperdon* and *Polytrichum* resp. 470.000 and 19.000 km, for the diaspores of *Taraxacum officinale*, *Picea abies*, *Pinus sylvestris* and *Fraxinus excelsior* resp. 10, 0.3, 0.5 and 0.02 km. The double distance can seldom be surpassed. With the same wind velocity, dispersal limits for other diaspores can be calculated by means of the equation Vg : x = (Sx) : (Sb). In this Vg is the known limit of a known diaspore, X the one to be determined, Sx the fall velocity of the latter and Sb the fall velocity of the known diaspore.

When a diaspore becomes detached at a higher wind velocity only (a factor of ecological importance), the distance increases with the square.

FEEKES (1936) checked for some anemochores in a newly drained, open polder some formulas of SCHMIDT for absolute distances and fall-velocities, not to be reproduced here. His results in the field agreed with expectations and showed some limitation for the distance reached, for instance in *Aster tripolium* one of 5 km. He admitted that incidental plus variants may obtain higher results, a fact which is also ecologically important.

MÜLLER-SCHNEIDER (1955), from whom the foregoing is partly derived, gives tables of various aerodynamical data. The dynamics are interesting in the special group of the wind ballists, intermediate between anemochory and autochory.

The factor of exposure is important. The negative influence of humidity on wind-dispersal requires auxiliary mechanisms for exposure at the right time. The opening in dry air only (xerochasy) is already apparent in anemochorous species of *Pinus*, but not in other species. The opposite effect, viz. opening after wetting (hygrochasy), is important in some desert-plants, where rain is beneficial.

In grasses, anemophilous and anemochorous exposure at the end of culms coincide. The relation to open plains is evident. In other cases, dispersal requires its own structures for exposure, for example, in some low-growing orchids where extreme elongation of the pedicel occurs after anthesis. In many epiphytic orchids, exposure of the seeds to the wind is brought about by elater-like hygroscopic hairs that gradually push the seeds out of the fruit (see Fig. 17). ULBRICH (1928) considers this as just a loosening up, but I found real ejection in *Taeniophyllum*. In *Dendrobium crumenatum*, I found that the seeds in the baccate but dehiscent fruit appear as lumps of twisted seeds. The seeds themselves untwist with lively movements when drying.

As to the distances reached, RIDLEY (pp. 3—10) gives some values for distances covered during storms, which I shall not repeat. MÜLLER-SCHNEIDER (1955) presented some verified data for such situations (recorded in kilometers): *Abies* 7, *Pinus sylvestris* 2, *Betula* 1,6, *Acer* 4, *Fraxinus excelsior* 1/2. Others have found: *Tussilago* 14, *Populus* 30, *Senecio congestus* 200. WOLFENBARGER (1959) gave a confused paper full of data on everything living. The extremes given do count, even though the dilution-effect should not be neglected.

Too distant a dispersal of single diaspores brings problems as to establishment of the species. Some orchid seeds from the West-Indies are blown to Florida, where they grow into plants but are doomed to a sterile life for lack of pollinators, as Dr. C. H. DODSON wrote me. There are other limits to extension of area by means of an anemochorous apparatus (as we shall see in our discussion of colonization and establishment on p. 89), but that Krakatau harboured anemochorous plants a few years after the eruption is a fact that cannot be reasoned away by the far-fetched objection that nobody has seen the seeds fly and settle.

Origins and backgrounds of anemochory are just as manifold as they are in anemophily of flowers, a phenomenon which also appears in a great number of zoophilous groups. In ancient Gymnosperms, anemochorous sidelines had already begun to develop. In Angiovulates the change-over may be located in the seed or in the fruit.

The uniformity of small anemochorous seeds in orchids goes back to terrestrial, ancestral forms like *Apostasia*. The condition may be connected with mycotrophy and the ensuing diminished chance of finding a suitable substrate.

In Compositae (see p. 130), the origin is connected with the emergence of single-seeded fruits, even in high trees (*Vernonia* spp.). In primitive Ranales, anemochory is practically absent; in "Amentiferae" it is scattered and has a secondary character.

We have seen that, in most cases, the two spheres of life, pollination (microspore dispersal) and seed-dispersal are strictly separate things that do not mix. In orchids they are even radically opposite in character. In the anemochorous Compositae, only a few switched to wind pollination for their flowers; in the anemophilous Cyperaceae, only a few to anemochory. In some incidentally deviating species with wind-flowers in diverse families, there is concurrence of the two spheres, as evidenced by species of *Poterium* (Rosaceae), *Thalictrum* (Ranunculaceae), *Hardwickia* (Leguminosae), and *Fraxinus* (Oleaceae). This concurrence is not so evident in incidentally deviating wind-dispersed species, indicating that the change to anemochory is obviously less profound.

Before starting a review of subclasses according to the behaviour of diaspores, it is necessary to point out that much dispersal by wind is incidental, especially during storms, and is not based on any special structure. Diaspores may cling to dead leaves or may (e. g.) be blown over plains and ice while forming part of various structures. Wind also exerts an influence on floating diaspores, so that the classification that will be given below might be complemented with "swimmers".

The dividing up of adapted forms between subclasses serves mostly to bring some descriptive order into the manifold structures whose function is to enlarge the surface. The resulting classification does not have such a pronounced ecological-evolutionary character as those in the other chapters, and the same is true of the agent. I use some terms from MÜLLER-SCHNEIDER and quote ULBRICH frequently; both authors gave fuller descriptive documentation of greater morphological interest.

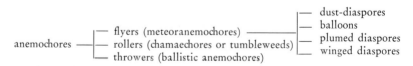

2. Dust-Diaspores

As previously stated, the apparent return to spores manifested in this group may in many cases have a relation with physiology and with the multitude of diaspores necessary for them to be omnipresent and to discover the special substrate that limits the distribution. Saprophytes, mycophytes, and ordinary parasites are dominant in the list of families with spore-like diaspores: Orchidaceae, Pirolaceae, Orobanchaceae, Scrophulariaceae, Balanophoraceae, Burmanniaceae, Sarraceniaceae, Droseraceae, Nepenthaceae. Weights for some species from the first three families were given as 0,003; 0,004, and 0,001 mg respectively.

We find very small seeds also in other groups, e. g. in some Crassulaceae, Caryophyllaceae *(Gypsophila, Sagina)*, Campanulaceae, *Eucalyptus,* and *Rhododendron.* In some cases a link with epiphytic life is present, also in tropical Gesneriaceae.

The small, flat (scobiform) diaspores of many species are a transition to winged diaspores.

3. Balloons

In the already small-seeded Orchidaceae and others, the loose testa assists in forming a balloon, but usually this feature is associated with fruits. The inflated and indehiscent pods of *Colutea arborescens* (a steppe plant) and of species of *Anthyllis* first spread over a short distance through the air, away from the mother plant, to proceed subsequently as tumbleweeds. Some *Trifolium* species have blown-up calyces or form balloon-heads by other means. There is also a transition to rollers in Polygonaceae *(Pterostegia* and *Harfordia)* by means of bracteoli, and in Chenopodiaceae from steppes with the aid of inflated bracteoli *(Atriplex vesicarium)* or perianth *(Kochia* and *Suaeda).* Some Umbelliferae from the steppes possess cavities in the pericarp *(Cachrys* and *Prengos).* Balloon fruits are known from Sapindaceae *(Cardiospermum),* Rosaceae *(Physocarpus),* and Scrophulariaceae *(Physocalyx).*

In some grasses as well as in hops *(Humulus),* the infructescence is balloon-like, but the separate fruit-bracts are more or less flat. Some *Anemone* species have groups of plumed achenes that can adhere to form a balloon.

4. Plumed (comose) Diaspores

Except for epiphytes, possession of plumed seeds or fruits is again rare in forests, frequent in open vegetations. In seeds a simple start on this way is elongation into one long hair *(Trichosporum).* Seeds of *Lephaimos* (a saprophytic member of the Gentianaceae) produce one hair from the long funicle and another one in the opposite position by elongation of the integument.

In Asclepiadaceae and Apocynaceae, a tuft apparently arises from a split-up wing, perhaps also in some Malvales. In Bromeliaceae *(Tillandsia)*, the tuft is of intricate origin, perhaps (as in other cases) derived from an arilloid. The hairs of *Salix* and *Populus* are outgrowths of the placenta, even arising in close association with unfertilized ovules.

Seed hairs may sometimes serve the purpose of enlarging the surface for hydrochory (see p. 63). Some plumed seeds float regularly on the tuft *(Bombax munguba)* and are then eaten by fish. The ecology of the seed-wool of *Gossypium* and *Ochroma* needs investigation in order to answer the question whether it is more significant for wind- or water-dispersal (STEPHENS, 1958).

In fruits, a simple solution is the persistence of the style(s) which eventually bear hairs (diverse Ranunculaceae, some Rosaceae such as species of *Geum* and *Dryas*). Steppe-grasses (such as *Stipa* and *Aristida*) develop long, hairy awns, which may acquire collateral functions such as boring and attachment to animals. Even pods of Leguminosae may develop anemochorous plumes *(Adesmia)*. Especially the calyx-pappus of Compositae may show hygroscopic movement, which has the function of regulating the moment of dispersal. Curiously, a number of Composites (a. o. *Lasiospermum)* abolish the pappus and develop achenes that are hairy all over.

5. Winged Flyers

Flat wings provide the means for gliding or, when one-sided, for dynamic propulsion. In both cases, they can function in diaspores much heavier than those in the previous class, but heaviness of necessity limits the distance and requires launching from a tree or a high climber.

First, seeds. The most famous, giant seed-wings (15 cm and very light) are found in *Macrozanonia macrocarpa,* a cucurbitaceous climber in tropical forests. One may doubt the effectiveness within the forest, but RIDLEY cites arrival on a ship at sea. High up in the canopy there may be turbulence. Many Bignoniaceae have large, winged seeds, for example *Oroxylum indicum* in Malesian light forest and *Pithecoctenium* in tropical America.

The wing of many Abietinae is a detached part of the fruiting scales, not part of the seed. Data concerning the ordinary "range" of the seeds (40—800 meter) are known, but exceptional longer traveling distances are important. In some Sterculiaceae *(Pterygota)*, the wing is clearly a transformation of an arilloid testa, a fact which also is apparent in other arillate groups with incidental wings (Meliaceae, Bombacaceae, and Celastraceae such as *Lophopetalum*), and in some African leguminous high trees belonging to the Piptadenieae. In some cases the wing is a lateral expansion of the funicle or a web between its loops (some Hippocrateaceae, Ixonanthaceae, Proteaceae). Winged fruits are very effective in the cases of *Alnus* and *Betula*, where they are small.

The one-winged propelling type is called samara, best known from *Acer*. Its aerodynamics and a comparison with the construction of an airplane wing need not be discussed here. The type occurs in a wide range of families, including the Leguminosae. The wing is apical in *Pterolobium* and basical in *Myroxylon* (reversed samara). In *Centrolobium robustum* (Brazil) the wing is 17 cm long. Many *Pterocarpus* and *Dalbergia* species have a circular wing around the pod. In *Erythrina lithosperma,* the pod dehisces and each valve with adhering seeds forms a samara, refound at some kilometers from an isolated tree. *Daniellia* (Tropical Africa) has a queer fruit with the separated endocarp rolled up and the seed dangling underneath. It is said to rotate during wind-dispersal, but I have my doubts about this as it stays too long on the tree and as the seed bears a small aril. Even in Magnoliaceae, carpids can become dry samaras *(Liriodendron)*.

Some fruits develop several wings on their sides, which again results in the production of rotating diaspores. Very impressive are those of *Cavanillesia* (Bombacaceae), high Amazonian trees, where the wings are up to 9 cm wide. The type also occurs in *Piscidia* (Leguminosae) and even in low-growing Polygonaceae (*Rheum* and *Rumex* species).

Fig. 16. Infructescences of Spinifex squarrosus on a shore in Java

Such side wings are often formed by accessory parts contributed by the flower. In *Triplaris surinamensis,* the originally white wings from the perianth crown the fruit as in a shuttlecock. The accessory wing of *Tilia* is formed from a bract, those of *Petraea volubilis* from the calyx, of *Congea velutina* from bracts. In the latter two, well known in tropical gardens, the coloured wings first collaborate in attracting animals for pollination.

The function of the calyx-wings of Dipterocarpaceae in South-Asian forests has long been under discussion. The weight of the diaspores (up to 30 g) and general experience are objections to the acceptance of common anemochory in the forest which, in addition, is rather windless. RIDLEY found them usually no more than 10 m away from the mother-trunk, rarely 30 m. The incidental aggregation in pure stands is perhaps a consequence. Seeds from more isolated trees of a *Shorea* species were, after a storm, found to have covered 400 meters, but these seeds do not germinate in the open. Like RIDLEY, HEINTZE (1932/35 on pp. 186—194) collected quite a literature on the subject. It has been assumed that the wings, after the seed has fallen, can provide the special position required for germination, but this has also been denied.

The wings on the fruits of *Begonia* and *Dioscorea* species have no direct dispersal-effect as these fruits are not detached. They may help the wind in shaking the fruit, an activity needed for the liberation of the small anemochorous seeds. Presentation merges into dispersal, as is also the case elsewhere.

6. Tumbleweeds

Scientific terms for the process of dispersal through tumbling are chamae-(anemo)chory (chamai = on the ground) and anemo-geochory. Especially here, the diaspores may consist of large parts of plants or even whole individuals that are or become globular. In windswept steppe regions tumbleweeds are frequent, and travellers there have described how their dwellings were overrun by masses of rolling plant material.

The special modifications are the curving up of flat parts and detachment devices of those parts or plants. The reversal of the hygroscopic curving up after moistening, so well known for the "Rose of Jericho", can result in anchoring by flattening in a favourable spot, accompanied by liberation of seeds. This famous name refers to *Anastatica hierochuntia* (Cruciferae) of the Near East and North Africa. Because of its opening and closing branch system, the whole dead plant is sold by florists, but other plants (*Selaginella* species) are often substituted for it in the trade, as is the Composite *Odontospermum pygmaea*.

Already in 1887, VOLKENS denied the old story of the rolling of *Anastatica* and STOPP (1958 b) complained that the plant only rolls in the literature (even in RIDLEY and ULBRICH) since in reality the tap-root is too tough to break off, so that the uncurling is only the hygrochastic presentation device after rain so common in semi-desert plants. Other local observers, however, confirmed the rolling away and the accumulation of the plants in depressions, stating that the tough tap-root has no laterals and can sometimes be torn out by the wind. Another plant from dry Mediterranean regions also has the reputation of a roller; viz. *Plantago cretica*. ZOHARY (1927) denied this, admitting only the curling up and uncurling of the fruiting axes as in *Anastatica*. The same rash generalization has been made in herbaria for inflated pods of *Crotalaria,* that are not detached at all. Other inflated pods (of *Colutea*), as discussed under balloons, do detach and roll. NORDHAGEN (1936 a) reports that even some dehiscing pods of northern *Astragalus* species can roll away; such pods possess devices for keeping the seeds in place during the process. Some *Medicago* pods, spiralized into balls, may also be rollers, although most are hooked and perhaps epizoochorous.

Physalis species with their light, inflated calyces are not simple rollers, either. The enclosed fruit is ornithochorous and detachment is doubtful, so that at best diplochory may be assumed. The related genus *Przewalskia* has fruit-calyces that are more likely to act as tumblers, and the same holds for some species of *Hibiscus* and *Pavonia* from African steppes with inflated, globular calyces (ULBRICH). In the Mediterranean region, the curious *Fedia cornucopiae* (Valerianaceae), to be discussed later (p. 83), has globular infructescences that break off easily and roll. In the thistle-like Composite *Gundelia tournefortii* of the same region, the whole plant behaves in this fashion and so does the American plant *Psoralea argophylla,* which has an abscission-joint at the base. North America has many more tumbleweeds in some Amaranthaceae and Chenopodiaceae *(Cycloma)* and in the introduced

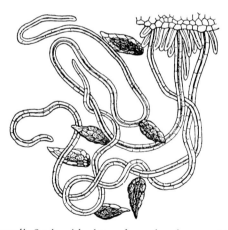

Fig. 17. Anguloa roezli. Seeds with elaters from the placenta. (After VELENOVSKY)

species *Salsola kali*. On Indonesian shores and in Australian steppes, the round infructescences of the grass *Spinifex* (see Fig. 16) are known as "windballs". The shore species S. *littoreus (squarrosus)* also endures sea transport (like *Salsola kali*). It has to be analysed, case for case, whether the whole

complexes stay together (synaptospermy) until a favourable spot is reached
or whether parts or loose diaspores are shed during the voyage. FEEKES
(1936) reported the latter for rolling complexes of *Suaeda maritima* and
Chenopodiaceae in an open, new polder, leaving long lines of seedlings
afterwards.

In some species of *Stipa* the long awns can secondarily form globes by
intertwining.

It seems unnecessary to translate and introduce the many terms of
HUTH, ULBRICH and HEINTZE for all kinds of rolling and flying anemochores or those for anemochores that are incidentally moved over snow fields.

7. Wind-Ballists (anemoballists)

The subject of wind-ballists is rather neglected in current handbooks.
It concerns plants with jacitation, a throwing mechanism which is put into
action by wind, in contrast to autonomous ballists and those that are worked
by rain or by passing animals (see later under autochory).

The best-known contrivance is the "censer-mechanism" of *Papaver*,
where the long, elastic pedicels swing to and fro in strong winds and the
capsules broadcast the seeds (through apical pores) over quite a distance.
For *P. somniferum*, ULBRICH measured distances of up to 15 meters. The
seeds are much heavier than those in censers constructed just for exposure
to wind. Many Campanulaceae are comparable, also with pores at the top
so that a simple falling-out in the absence of a strong wind is prevented.
The same situation occurs in many Caryophyllaceae and species of *Scrophularia* and *Antirrhinum,* and perhaps in *Primula veris.*

According to MÜLLER-SCHNEIDER, the long, tough peduncle of *Bellis
perennis,* helped by the postfloral shape of the torus, can throw out the
pappus-less achenes when swinging.

J. Water and Hydrochory

1. General

According to HEINTZE (p. 18), the term "hydatochory" of ULBRICH and
followers goes back to a slip of the pen of ENGLER.

Water plays a limited role in land plants and an important one in plants
of swamps and shores, although the relation is far from general as many
"sea-grasses" and Juncaceae, Cyperaceae rely on animals (ducks, fishes)
and on wind.

In some cases the seeds sink but the liberated seedling can help out by
floating for short-range dispersal.

When present, the connection with water is clearly utilization, derived
from all possible other conditions. It is practically absent in Gymnosperms

(for the case of *Cycas* see p. 81). Even in families such as the Hydrocharitaceae, basically returned to water life, the general hydrochory is of a
secondary nature. In general, they stick to old modes for pollination, but
dispersal seems to be changed more easily. The number of aquatic plants
which have switched to dispersal by water is much larger than those switched
to pollination by means of water.

The still more aquatic family of the Podostemonaceae has also maintained insect-pollination (and seed-setting) in the air, both processes taking
place when the water is low in the dry season. WILLIS (see RIDLEY) already
reported for Ceylon that the seeds of *Lawia* become mucilaginous when
wetted and may stick to the feet of birds walking over the rocks. In Vene-
zuelan species of *Rhyncholaxis* and *Mourera*, GESSNER and HAMMER (1962)
saw very fast mucilage formation; they think that this serves the purpose
of anchoring seeds to rocks, a process which in this case is demonstrably
effective even in streaming water. An objection against direct water-dispersal is that at this period the water level is said to be far below the level
where the plants are ultimately found attached, which is the highest level
ever reached by the water. ACCORSI (1953) interpreted the situation for some
species (of *Apinagia, Mourera, Meniopsis,* and *Tristicha*) as merely a new
establishment on the same spot by the mucilage — atelechory in a dangerous
environment. He observed germination to take place mostly at the beginning
of the rain-period in or on the open fruit, from where the seedings fall on
the rock, subsequently to be attached by hapters. The place of attachment
was below flood level.

Because of their secondary, incidental and convergent character, it is
difficult to describe concisely the structural modifications of hydrochory.
We have already seen that they are often based on anemochory. The two
have in common a connection with an abiotic, wasteful and unselective
agent, working with weight and surface area. Hydrochory shows a diver-
sification paralleling that of anemochory; the submerged diaspores can be
compared with flyers, and the floating ones with rollers, while ballistic
hydrochores also exist. However, the subdivision of the class adopted here
has to pay some attention to the special nature of water as an agent. The
presentation of the diaspores is also comparable. Many hydrochores bend
their fruit-stalks down (*Cabomba, Victoria, Hydrocharitaceae*), whereas in
Nuphar (not purely hydrochorous) the seeds mature above water. The
following scheme presents a functional review.

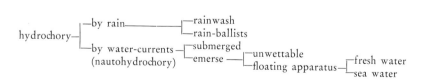

2. Rain Wash (Ombrohydrochory)

In this group (ombros = rain) we find unspecialized plants owing their dispersal to rain, which flushes the diaspores away over some distance. The phenomenon has rarely been analyzed. RIDLEY (p. 165) observed it in the rain forest and in botanical gardens for small, low-growing plants with diaspores too heavy for wind dispersal. Mountain streams can complete the action, carrying the diaspores to unusually low, temporary habitats.

The exposure to rain is often promoted by hygrochasy, the opening of containers in a humid atmosphere. Many swamp plants rely on this opening mechanism for floating seeds, too (*Caltha, Veronica* spp.). Curiously, the phenomenon has some limited importance for short-range dispersal in arid regions with occasional showers. There, some open leguminous pods ("Rinnenhülse") as well as the fruits of *Sedum acre* and of some Mesembryanthemaceae open in rain and let the seeds go without further devices. The distance is, however, so small that the main aspect involved is the holding of seeds for germination until the rains come.

ZOHARY (1937) reports that the cruciferous fruits of *Leptaleum filifolium* also open at well-defined times as a "Rinnenhülse" (fruit with open groove). It is uncertain whether the rare rains have a dispersal effect in some desert Compositae such as the *Geigeria*, described by STOPF (1958). The dry involucrum is folded over the fruiting heads until rain comes. The Rose of Jericho perhaps also belongs here (see p. 58). Investigators in North American deserts ascribe farther dispersal to rain floods over hard-baked surfaces.

3. Rain-Ballists

In a small group of plants we find a repetition of the splash-cup mechanism, where falling raindrops provide the energy to make diaspores jump out of cups. In Fungi and Hepaticae it is not rare.

MÜLLER-SCHNEIDER (1955) separated the group from KERNER's old group of ballists. In the newly created category, raindrops make a lever mechanism swing back and throw the seeds out of containers. The horizontally oriented pods of some species of *Iberis* and *Thlaspi* (Cruciferae) catch the impact of raindrops well. For *T. perfoliatum*, MÜLLER-SCHNEIDER mentions a throw of 80 cm. In some Labiatae the throwing is said to be done by the concave upper lip of the calyx (e. g. in some species of *Ocimum, Prunella*, and *Scutellaria*). BRODIE (1955) devoted papers to the phenomenon. His assumption concerning *Hyptis suaveolens* does not tally with my experience (see p. 67). NORDHAGEN (1936 a, b) criticized the creation of this category (see p. 73), but I could confirm experimentally MÜLLER's observations in *Aethionema*. The fruits show at the same time hygrochasy and the seeds myxospermy in *A. saxatile*.

4. Submerged Transport in Water

Many aquatic plants possess diaspores that are not appreciably lighter than water, especially some marine Helobiae and species of *Callitriche*. They are nevertheless transported by currents, assisted by some enlargement of surface by means of hairs *(Peplis portula, Nymphoides orbiculata)*. In *Nymphaea alba*, and *Euryale*, the seeds even float for a shorter or longer time on a transformed, ancestral arilloid. The hairs of *Limnanthemum (Nymphoides) nymphaeoides* cause flotation as long as they are filled with air, but can also serve as hooks. In the Acanthaceae some riverside species *(Hygrophila)* have adpressed seed hairs, that are erected in water to form a slimy mass.

In this type and the following one, some atelechorous mechanisms prevent too long-lasting a displacement, just as in the case of wind-dispersed steppe plants. Usually it is the disintegration of the swimming apparatus that causes anchoring in the mud. In *Aponogeton* the testa bursts. Sometimes, anchoring hooks help in final fixation and establishment; this is true also for the originally floating fruits of *Trapa natans*, the water chestnut. The hooks on the seeds of *Barclaya* (a Malaysian water lily) probably serve primarily this purpose, although they can also adhere to water-visiting animals. ULBRICH (1928) lists some water-burrs (see our Fig. 20), a. o. species of *Zostera* and *Ceratophyllum*. Even some vegetative, seed-like, winter-buds of aquatic plants (e. g. of *Cymodocea antarctica)* possess such anchors. The sharp spines on the dehiscing fruit of *Victoria amazonia* are (like those on its leaves and stalks) purely protective (against vegetarian water-animals), without significance for durinanology and dispersal.

The large, floating, free seedlings of *Amphibolis* (p. 95) are enclosed in a spinous structure.

As an appendix, which might be placed anywhere in this sub-chapter, I give a list of water and waterside plants dispersed (also) in the seedling phase, hovering in currents or floating on the surface: *Lythrum salicaria*, species of *Juncus, Hottonia, Mimulus luteus, Primula japonica, Stachys palustris, Scrophularia aquatica, Aster tripolium, Salicornia herbacea, Enalus acoroides*. The cases of *Inga* and mangrove plants are dealt with elsewhere.

5. Floating Diaspores

The first, rather accidental, possibility for floating is that small seeds are unwettable and float on the surface of water, taking advantage of the surface tension. The cause can be the chemical constitution of the testa or the small pits in it, filled with trapped air. A tropical instance is *Isotoma longiflora*. When submerged, the seeds sink. MÜLLER-SCHNEIDER adds: *Ranunculus repens, Myosotis scorpioides, Cirsium palustre*.

The most frequent cause of floating is low specific weight, achieved by air spaces, lightness of albumen or cotyledons, or corky tissues. In fresh water this is sufficient equipment; protection is superfluous. Often the potentially protective layers are shed. Loss of dormancy and immediate germination occur, perhaps to be explained causally by disappearance of inhibiting factors. See the list of seedlings above.

Lotos fruits *(Nelumbium)* attain, after having been desiccated, a prolonged dormancy (of some centuries). The persisting receptacle breaks off and floats. The loosened nuts float, sink and emerge again, producing (at least in *N. lutea*) floating seedlings.

There is no reason to list many cases, as few principles are involved. Often the low specific weight is entirely fortuitous, as the plant has no natural relation with open water. PRAEGER (1913) analyzed buoyancy in British plants.

In the aquatic group of the Helobiae some have dehiscing fruits as diaspores, others fallen-off seeds, which may or may not float; one-seeded achenes are often found. In Carices and grasses *(Glyceria, Coix, Oryza)*, glumes and other bracts assist. Wind and currents help in the transport. Dispersal here is in harmony with the habitat, though many riverside plants are not entirely bound to water-transport. Among such species of *Sonchus*, *S. palustris* developed best collateral floating power. As the genus is primarily anemochorous the establishment in the specific habitat rests on factors other than dispersal. Sometimes inland races of the same species differ in buoyancy, showing the relatively recent action of selection. RIDLEY (p. 240) commented on the rarity of hydrochorous Cyperaceae *(Mariscus)*.

All this refers to plants connected with pools and quiet streams, not with fast-flowing rivers and torrents. In the latter the fluviatile hydrochory provides only downward transport, so that upward dispersal remains a riddle and overland transport by birds must be invoked (cf. Podostemonaceae, p. 61). In this connection a warning is necessary that plant-sociologists, interested in distribution, use the term "fluviatile plants" in a different sense, namely for species which enter a region along river valleys or are restricted to the latter.

Flowing rivers carry much "drift" of diaspores, but this transport is mostly ineffectual as many drift-seeds are dead or doomed to death. GUPPY (1906) dealt with river-drift too, mentioning e. g. *Dioclea reflexa* from river-banks as spread by water, but most of the drifting seeds are already dead on reaching the sea. STOPP (1956) analysed (with the same result) the drift of the Congo river. He refers to other cases, also the fossil ones that trouble paleontologists. The frequent occurrence of dry-land plants such as *Mucuna, Entada,* and *Physostigma* tallies with the results of studies on the marine drift (see below). I fear that STOPP sees things too black-and-white, as some of the dead diaspores are really hydrochorous and die only after too long a stay in water.

In tropical forests there are species which frequent riversides and have fruits adapted to river-transport; in South America, e. g. *Grias cauliflora* and species of *Combretum,* whose seeds are dead when they finally reach the sea. For Malesia, I cite species of *Hodgsonia, Pangium edule, Gluta renghas,* and the stenophyllous *Eugenia salictoides.* The sea-dispersed *Barringtonia* species can be seen as derived from river-dispersed species, like *B. spicata.* The same goes for *Calophyllum inophyllum* and the riverine *C. macrocarpa.* ULBRICH mentions *Fiebrigiella gracilis* from Andine river shores. *Mimosa asperata* belongs here, too. RIDLEY deals with this group separately on pp. 197—241, including *Hevea brasiliensis.*

In sea water, a much more aggressive substrate in which a much longer stay can be expected, the floating apparatus has to be more sophisticated. The dispersal mostly concerns land plants, some of which, are more or less tolerant of salt. An impermeable layer protecting the embryo is present in most cases. In the giant drupe of *Cocos nucifera,* this layer (endocarp) was present in its organizational type; the fibrous mesocarp serves for floating and the endosperm has in its "milk" a provision for establishment on a shore without much fresh water. This can be seen as a beginning of vivipary. The "nut" germinates above ground, a process promoted by rainwater penetrating into the abraded husk. A number of temperate shore plants also are dispersed by sea *(Cakile maritima, Crambe maritima, Lathyrus maritimus);* furthermore, many halophytes from tidal mud. *Aster tripolium* has become diplochorous, being dispersed originally by wind but secondarily by the floating of achenes and seedlings. This rarely serves for long-range dispersal. The same is true even of reduced, marine aquatics of the *Zostera*-type, though *Zostera* itself can endure a long stay in salt water.

The tropical sea drift contains many diaspores with full vitality. The classical description is the one by SCHIMPER (1891). Others, a. o. GUPPY (1906) investigated for many instances the time span over which the vitality is retained in sea water. The best-known seeds, washed ashore even on European beaches, are of the adventitious type of hard seeds of *Entada, Mucuna, Cassia fistula,* which are also found in fluviatile drift. The seeds are mostly dead and the living ones rarely germinate or grow on the sea shore. The famous *Lodoicea seychellarum* belongs in this group. The giant nuts do not float when fresh. Most of the viable drift diaspores belong to shore plants from the mangrove-or *Barringtonia* formation; of the genus *Mucuna,* only *M. gigantea.*

We shall not discuss all details, but mention the curious seeds of *Caesalpinia (Guilandina) bonduc* and *C. bonducella* (Leguminosae). They look like pebbles, are extremely hard and can float for years, thus providing an almost pantropical distribution. For the influence of sea currents see GUPPY (1917). Some indehiscent, anemochorous, winged pods of species of *Dalbergia* and some hard joints of loments (jointed pods) of *Desmodium* species could easily change to hydrochory in shore-dwelling species. Among the Compositae, only a few have switched to sea-dispersal. The best known is *Wedelia biflora,* with a corky pericarp and no pappus. A peculiar case is that of *Thuarea sarmentosa,* a grass of sea sands on Pacific islands. It has one female spikelet at the base of the rachis, which folds over it, becomes thick and hard and forms a protecting and floating cover over the caryops. *Hernandia peltata,* a seashore tree, has a fleshy, open cup formed by the calyx around the fruit; the latter floats on it, although it can also float by itself. The cup has primarily another function, as we shall see for many cases of transitional, polychorous beach plants in the sub-chapter on poly-chory.

We may finally return to the coconut, a favorite subject in discussions on origin and dispersal. Against RIDLEY and others who emphasized loss of viability after prolonged stay in salt water, but with the support of other botanists such as BÜNNING and DOCTERS VAN LEEUWEN, it must be main-tained that the tree is actually sea-dispersed in Indonesia and over certain Pacific Islands, where it germinates and grows spontaneously as a native behind the floodline (cf. Fig. 21) but is of course lacking when the population and animals collect or destroy the nuts.

We have now met sufficient proof (already presented by RIDLEY, p. 250) that hydrochores, especially on the sea-shore, are a mixed crowd, derived from inland plants. This does not preclude the possibility that a reverse, later evolution can also have occurred, as GUPPY argued. We shall find support for this idea in the part on island floras.

In this field we find again that dispersal is but one of the factors determining the presence of plants. In tropical salt-marshes *Pluchea indica* is wind-dispersed. Many beach plants are bound to the sandy shore merely by virtue of being xerophytic plants, tolerant of salt. *Spinifex* and *Tribulus* (see p. 67) are examples of this, as are the aloes and cacti found as adven-tives on tropical beaches. We already discussed *Sonchus* and *Aster tripolium* on tidal flats, where *Statice* species are immigrants from steppe regions. These forms are primarily anemochorous, already more or less halophilous.

K. Epizoochory, Transport on the Outside of Animals in General

1. Diverse Origins

The term exozoochory is also in use for diaspores with adhesive me-chanisms (spines, hooks or viscid exudates), which detach easily from the mother plant and are mostly placed near ground level.

In seeds the phenomenon is rather rare, especially in the early phase of fruit development where the seed dominates in dispersal *(Barclaya).* In

Luzula species and some derived Leguminosae (species of *Erythrophloeum* and *Clitoria*) the viscid exudation seems a secondary device for further transport, as in the Podostemonaceae. These instances are in some cases combined with explosion and active deposition of the seeds on passing animals; this is also true for *Ecballium,* some species of *Oxalis,* and some Acanthaceae (see under autochory). The viscid substance adhering to seeds of some water plants *(Ottelia, Hydrocharis)* may be primarily hydrochorous, although it may also stick to the feet of waterfowl, as discussed before.

The intricate situation, to be analyzed functionally in each single case, is further complicated by the presence of mucilage after wetting of the seeds of non-aquatics. This mucilage functions primarily in establishment (see p. 94), but in the case of *Plantago* species it also has an effect for epizoochory. The field is full of simple utilization, in accordance with its lateness. In Labiatae the mucilaginous epidermis of the nutlets stands in relation with germination and is generally well protected against premature wetting by hairs in the throat of the calyx and by opening of the calyx at the time of liberation only. In Java, however, I found that the calyx of *Hyptis suaveolens* is wide open at maturity, exposing the two nutlets to rain. This deviation is not incidental and accidental; the swelling causes one nutlet to come out while the other remains inside, and the calyx separates easily. The reduction to two nuts is significant.

In fruits of all morphological types, adhesive mechanisms are so varied that classification is meaningless. Sometimes *(Forskahlea* in African steppes) even hooked vegetative parts, that can root, are a means of dispersal. We may, however, point out the importance of some types and also tidy up some.

2. Trample Burrs

The class of "Trampelkletten" (trample burrs) of German authors, such as ULBRICH and MÜLLER-SCHNEIDER, contains hard burrs lying on the ground. MURBECK (1920) has pictured many, including the one-seeded ones of *Onobrychis viciifolia* and other queer synaptospermous leguminous pods *(Biserrula* and *Hippocrepis).* ASCHERSON founded the class after KERNER reported diaspores of a *Tribulus* (puncture-vine) as being present on the hoofs of sheep, even piercing them with claws, sharper and harder than in ordinary burrs. They are frequent in steppe regions and thus occur in families specialized for this habitat: Chenopodiaceae *(Bassia, Spinacia),* Zygophyllaceae *(Tribulus)* and Pedaliaceae *(Josephinia, Harpagophytum, Martynia),* also in some more Leguminosae (species of *Astragalus).* The Mediterranean form, *Emex spinosa* (Polygonaceae), has them, partly drawn underground as a transition to geocarpy; also *Neurada procumbens* (Rosaceae), where the hypanthium is flat, with spines on the fruiting side (Fig. 22). We meet here the double face of desert diaspores; spines for epizoochory as well as for anchoring. I found them in *Neurada* lying almost all with the spiny side down, well anchored, as MURBECK (1920) pictured them. In the text he speaks in one place about anchoring, in another about the seedlings piercing the flat side with tap roots when this is pressed against the soil. STOPP (1962), in the case of the Pedaliaceae, paid special attention to the aspect of anchoring (see p. 78) and expressed doubt concerning the burr nature of the diaspores, which I admit is mostly surmise.

3. Water Burrs

Even some hydrochores among Pedaliaceae *(Trapella)* show the claws, as in *Trapa;* here, they certainly cannot be trampled upon and clearly serve the purpose of anchoring only. ULBRICH concedes this and admits also that not all spiny fruits are adhesive, since adherence of such "water burrs" to fishes is improbable. We already discussed the group under hydrochory (Fig. 20).

4. Burrs

Some spiny infructescences, never dislodged from the mother plant, are known as shake- or rattle-burrs ("Schüttelkletten"). They will, in this book, be dealt with under "autochory" as a special kind of ballists. A warning not to rely for ecological conclusions on the mere presence of spines and hooks! Even RIDLEY misinterpreted the case of *Arctium (Lappa),* never detached.

The American cocklebur *(Xanthium)* really has an epizoochorous burr (female head only), readily passed to animals. Burrs are rare in primitive Ranales, frequent in weedy pioneers such as most of the Compositae. The adhesion is here not only obtained by a hooked pappus, as in *Bidens,* or by a hooked involucrum *(Xanthium). Siegesbeckia orientalis* has spread all over the tropical world by means of viscid bracts. Some South American weeds of this family found a queer detour: the pappus vanished, but the withered corolla took over as an epizoochorous hook. In *Adenocaulon,* the achenes themselves are covered with viscid glands. All this functional convergence goes far beyond the mere "utilization" presumed by GUPPY (p. 3).

In North America, *Solanum rostratum* is known as "buffalo-burr" because of the curious change of the berries of the genus into spiny burrs. The Gramineae have also produced some burrs, for instance in the austra-lianized small-burr-grass *(Tragus racemosus)* and some species of *Centho-theca, Spartina,* and *Echinolaena.*

In terminal, pioneering, weedy forms, the Leguminosae developed hooked and viscid pods and sometimes jointed pods, breaking up easily: species of *Desmodium* (Tick seed), *Medicago,* etc. When growing above ground level, they should be classed as burrs. The function of the spines with gum, on pods of *Sindora* (falling from high trees) is not clear; neither is it obvious in the case of the resin in the pericarp of *Trachylobium*.

The vegetative bulbils of *Remusatia vivipara,* living on rocks and in tree forks in tropical forests, are burrs. Further burrs are rare there, the forest grass *Leptaspis* has adhesive spikelets, the herb *Achyranthes aspera* small prickly burrs. The sticky fruit of *Pisonia* trees has been discussed already.

Pricking into and hooking in on fur are mixed with sticking on. The sharp beaks and spiny awns on diaspores of some grasses and Cyperaceae *(Rhynchospora)* stand apart as a more boring type, penetrating into the fur of mammals. The limits between this type, that with anemochorous awns, and the boring one of *Erodium* (see p. 95) are not sharply defined. Many *Stipa* species use both methods of transport and some *(S. setacea)* are a pest to sheep as the spikelets even penetrate into the skin.

5. Other Spiny Fruits

Many fruits, e. g., those of *Bixa*, *Nephelium* and *Datura,* low or high in morphology and taxonomy, fall (like *Arctium,* just discussed) into the category of acanthochores of DANSEREAU and LEMS (1957), though the spines have no direct relation with dispersal, at the most being of significance against being prematurely eaten. The cupule of *Castanea* and *Fagus,* not a fruit and not arillate, also belongs to this group, which seems to lie outside our field, just as the diabolical stinging pods of *Mucuna.*

Remains as an explanation "archaism". CROIZAT explains such outgrowths as remnants of "un-sexualised" scales between perianth and ovary. In inferior fruits like *Sechium* and *Victoria* this is difficult to visualize.

CORNER'S "Durian Theory" proclaims an a-morphological archaism.

The durian *(Durio zibethinus)* got its Indonesian name (the spiny thing) from the short, very hard spines on the fruit. In this case, some protective function is clear since at maturity the spines make access to the arilloids impossible to all but the largest mammals. In the "Durian Theory", how-

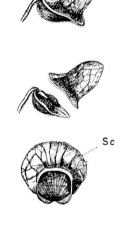

Fig. 18. Fruiting calyx of Scutellaria altissima. Sc scutellum. The upper figures from the side before and after dehiscence, the lower figures from the front, upper and lower part separated, keeping the nutlets in place. (From NORDHAGEN, 1936 b)

ever, (to be discussed on p. 113) the spininess is proclaimed to be a primitive archaism, a companion to primitive arilloids. This seems somewhat exaggerated, considering the above-mentioned spiny fruits and the fact that many really primitive fruits such as those of *Archidendron, Sterculia,* and *Paeonia* (see p. 111) lack spines. The only Sterculiacea I known to possess spines, has late, explosive fruits.

L. Autochory, Dispersal by the Plant Itself

1. General

Many authors considered it as evident that the treatment of dispersal methods should begin with those exerted by the plant itself. They combined the latter in one category, that of autochory, as opposed to all other methods which use some outside influence and are combined in the category of allochory. The term "active dispersal" is less fitting, considering the passive ballists to be discussed, where the demarcation from allochory is also not sharp and some outside influence is necessary.

Generative diaspores can also be spread somewhat by just growth, e. g. when stalked inflorescences curve down for presentation or when fruiting axes creep into fissures *(Linaria cymbalaria);* and when creeping stems drop seeds *(Polygonum aviculare)* or bury them (many geocarpous plants). Our concern is here with more active processes of autochory.

Autonomous self-dispersal is often just a further development of motions serving exposure or presentation of diaspores to some agent. We shall see this clearly in the explosion of late legumes and in some Rutaceae, where the endocarp first pushes out the seeds and in terminal cases propels them *(Esenbeckia* and *Metrodora* in KUHLMANN and KÜHN, 1947).

Explosive liberation of diaspores is, of course, an old feature. It is found in fungi and fern sporangia, mostly as a presentation to wind. It also occurs, as an escape, in spores, seedlings, and bulbils of species of *Lycopodium* and *Selaginella* (see p. 103). In the flowering plants the seeding organs had to rediscover it, which happened especially in the higher families. In the Annonaceae only one instance has been described. Autochory is frequent in arid regions.

The term "ballists" is generally used in Europe and also in the terminology of CLEMENTS and DANSEREAU. RIDLEY and followers prefer the (too vague) term of "mechanical dispersal". For our "passive ballists" CLEMENTS used the term "mortar-fruits".

We can discern several methods of autochory, partly according to structural differences, partly to ecological differences.

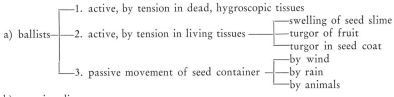

a) ballists
— 1. active, by tension in dead, hygroscopic tissues
— 2. active, by tension in living tissues —
  — swelling of seed slime
  — turgor of fruit
  — turgor in seed coat
— 3. passive movement of seed container —
  — by wind
  — by rain
  — by animals

b) creeping diaspores

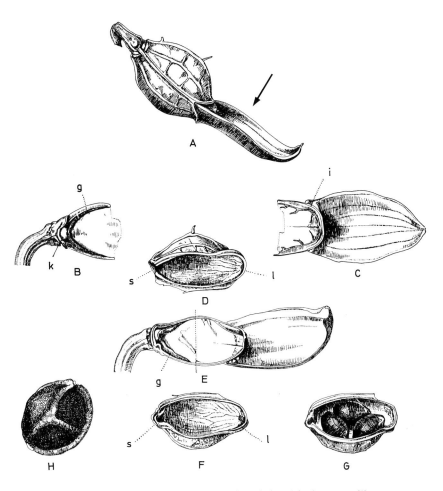

Fig. 19. Siliqua of Carrichtera annua. A — The whole with the spoon-like tangent from the sterile part, B — The springy part of the replum, remaining attached, C — The tangent and part of the replum broken-off at the ejaculation of the seeds. (From NORDHAGEN, 1936b)

2. Active Ballists

The term ballists (ballo = I throw) goes back to KERNER (1891). Later authors made subdivisions; most cases concern herbs, but trees are also included. The release of tension in dead tissues is best known from the classical legume. For a discussion of the mechanics involved, I refer to FAHN and ZOHARY (1955) and earlier authors. The tropical low tree *Bauhinia purpurea* is considered as holder of the record (15 meters). MÜLLER-SCHNEI-DER (1955) collected a list of distances.

In the Euphorbiaceae this kind of explosion is frequent, also in high trees *(Hevea)*, with the record of 14 meters for *Hura crepitans,* the sandbox tree. The mechanisms are different in species of *Geranium* (p. p.), *Viola* (p. p.), *Buxus, Dictamnus* (Rutaceae), *Montia (Claytonia)* (Portulacaceae), *Polygonum virginianum, Collomia* (Polemoniaceae), and *Alstroemeria* (an exception in Monocotyledones). Some owe their wide distribution as weeds to ballism. Some show a certain rhythm over the day.

The family of the Acanthaceae has special "jaculators", hard, elastic funicles *(Acanthus).* In species of *Ruellia* the fruits split after wetting of a weak spot and the ejected seeds have the coat of hairs mentioned for *Hygrophila* on p. 63. In the Cruciferae the siliqua can eject seeds after sudden loosening of the valves, sometimes with the assistance of a sucking force in the air (OVERBECK, 1925). Seeds of *Oxalis* and *Biophytum* have a turgid, outer testa, which splits and ejects the seeds over a distance of more than 2 meters. In some Moraceae *(Dorstenia)* apparently the same thing happens, but it is the small fruit which pinches the seed proper out. In the related forms *Pilea* and *Elatostema* (also forest herbs in the tropics), staminodes eject the whole, small fruit. Tension of the living fruit wall is the causative force in *Lathraea clandestina* and species of *Impatiens.* In the gourds *Elaterium* and *Cyclanthera* the endocarp plus placenta under pression of the mesocarp split the latter and uncurl suddenly, throwing the seeds out. In the squirting cucumber *(Ecballium elaterium),* the sticky pulp with the seeds is ejected by pressure. Cooperation of touching animals is sometimes needed here to release the tension and to transport seeds farther. This may be valid for the small loranthaceous parasite, *Arceuthobium,* where the viscid kernels are liberated explosively from the berry. The distance of 400 meters from the motherplant, mentioned in RIDLEY, may be due to such secondary bird-transport. We have found many more instances of secondary transport after explosion.

3. Passive Ballists

Ever since KERNER (1891), this group has often been designated as the ballists proper. The action of an outside agent does not just release internal tension, but itself provides the energy for the action. Often special structures transfer the energy in the desired way. If one considers the result only, the event may be treated also under the respective agents, as has been done here to some degree. The transferring structures are, however, too nicely convergent and too illuminating as to their function to permit omission of their curious morphology here.

First, there are wind-ballists swaying on long stalks. They have already been mentioned as ballistic anemochores on p. 60; KERNER also included pappusless Compositae, such as species of *Centaurea,* in this group.

For rain-ballists see p. 62.

Next come ballists operated by passing animals. NORDHAGEN (1936 a, 1936 b) distinguished these as tangent-ballists from anemochorous holoballists, where the shock acts on the whole plant. Some of them have shakeburrs which do not detach, but grip passing animals and return like a spring to their former position, ejecting the diaspores. Burdock *(Arctium* or *Lappa)* belongs here. Many Labiatae have infructescences shaped like globular balls, receiving shocks on protruding, hard calyx teeths. Some temperate species of *Salvia* show this and also tropical species of *Leonotis* and *Hyptis.* It is curious that such *Hyptis* spp. *(H. brevipes* and *H. rhomboides [capitata]),* have burr-like pseudo-heads and that their nuts do not produce the mucilage of *H. suaveolens* (see p. 67), a species with flowers that are plainly axillar. The demarcation from rain-ballists is to be determined after careful analysis of the following group, which possesses queerly deformed, more-specialized calyces. Some species of *Teucrium* and *Scutellaria,* also *Salvia glutinosa,* have a post-florally enlarged calyx with a springy pedicel and a kettle in which hairs keep the loose nutlets in position while at rest. In *Scutellaria altissima* the upper lip of the closed calyx has the tangent, the part receiving the shock, in its "scutellum". The whole upper lip is then thrown off the kettle along with the seeds (see Fig. 18), according to NORDHAGEN.

STOPP (1958 a) found the same type of queerly dehiscing fruiting calyx in ballistic species of *Aeolanthus* (a Congolese Labiate).

Teasel *(Dipsacus)* also belongs here, as does perhaps *Polygonum virginianum.* NORDHAGEN included some leguminous pods of Scandinavian *Oxytropis* species *(O. lapponica* and *O. deflexa),* where wind and raindrops are not able to operate the ballistic mechanism (humidity disturbs springiness) and where reindeer can dislodge the firmly arrested seeds. Also, species of *Tiarella* (Saxifragaceae), *Vella* and *Carrichtera* (Cruciferae) with queer siliquae (see Fig. 19), in which the sterile carpel has grown out as a tangent.

4. Creeping Diaspores

The hygroscopic bristles of many diaspores can, when dry and humid weather conditions alternate, perform movements. Insofar as this leads to penetration into the soil, so well known for *Erodium,* the phenomenon belongs in the chapter on establishment. In some species of *Trifolium* — as well as in many Dipsacaceae, Compositae, and Gramineae — the bristles

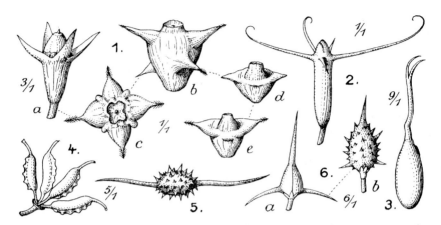

Fig. 20. Water-burrs. 1. Trapa natans, 2. Trapella sinensis, 3. Zostera marina, 4. Zanichellia palustris, 5. Blyxa echinosperma, 6a. Ceratophyllum demersum, 6b. C. submersum. (From ULBRICH, 1928)

Fig. 21. Coconut germinating on the shore of the new island Anak Krakatau among the drift, 10 years after origin of the island. Behind it Spinifex squarrosus. In the background young trees of Casuarina

of the anemochorous calyx-pappus or the awns produce by their movements some creeping of the whole (see Fig. 23). The pappus of some *Centaurea* species is too small for anemochory, but creeping helps in the seed dispersal in combination with ballistics and myrmecochory.

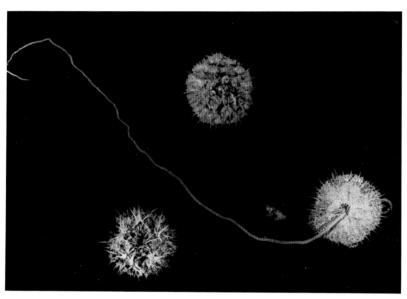

Fig. 22. Neurada procumbens. Woody, spiny hypanthia, one with lower, smooth surface up, showing taproot which has pierced opening. (Photo NATAN)

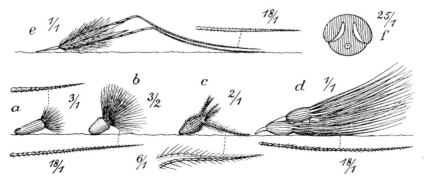

Fig. 23. Creeping diaspores, with the ends of the bristles magnified. Direction of movement to the left. a) Centaurea cyanus, b) Crupina vulgaris, c) Trifolium squarrosum, d) Aegilops ovata, e) Avena sterilis. (After ULBRICH, 1928)

M. Barochory, Dispersal by Weight Only

The term (from baros = heaviness) is not entirely satisfactory, implying that the diaspores have no other means of dispersal at all, but also that they can roll away by the impetus of their weight. What authors commonly place in this group is rather chaotic and incoherent (*Rhizophora, Quercus, Juglans*). MÜLLER-SCHNEIDER even places here some myrmecochores where the bending to the soil is just a presentation of diaspores to ants. Dropping of heavy pods for ruminants is also just presentation, not barochory.

The class forms one type of DANSEREAU and LEMS, which includes those cases where means of transport are only seemingly absent, in reality being just invisible. *Cocos* is also included here.

If we maintain the class, *Aesculus hippocastanum* is a convincing instance, (see p. 27) and also perhaps some large leguminous seeds as long as we find no properties indicating a specific agent. We may suspect that *Castanospermum australe* with its chestnut-like seeds is in this category; the diaspores seem barochorous, until we discover that not the diaspore but the parent-fruit is specialized — an efficient ballist. Another possible case is that of the South-American *Mora (Dimorphandra)*, which in *M. excelsa* exhibits one of the largest seeds in existence (12 × 7 cm). As it is flat, it does not roll, so that we find just no dispersal; achory (see p. 98). We shall study this abandonment of dispersal in favour of letting local seedlings wait for an opportunity, in the part on the rain-forest.

VI. Combination, Limitation and Cooperation

As is fitting to a textbook, we started with autecology, the study of the individual species in relation to certain environmental factors. We stressed clear-cut cases of relation with one specific factor, to allow an orderly review as well as the recognition of natural divisions. Although ecological principles were also presented, the pigeon-holes were necessary for general orientation.

It is now time to recognize coherently that this was an over-simplification, that in nature the environment works as a whole, that vegetations and their animal inhabitants are ecosystems with internal coordination; also, that each process has a counterpart which acts as a regulating brake and that in nature synecology is at work, with multiple internal connections.

A. Atelechory

1. General

This is the occasion to introduce a concept which has general importance, although it has usually been treated for one kind of vegetation only, the semi-desert. In contrast to the usual dispersal, which tries to reach far and to conquer new habitats, we now see (and will come to study) the avoidance of too much or any dispersal and the inhibitory mechanisms to obtain this.

The category may be called anti-telechory, atelechory or achory. Recently ZOHARY (1962), a specialist on the subject, switched to the term topochory. This means dispersal on the spot, which is a contradictio in terminis, so that his term might better be replaced by "achory", no dispersal. If he means to stress the liberation of diaspores on the spot, the radical "topo" should be used in the combination "topospory". Earlier, we were already forced to recognize the necessity of some atelechorous mechanisms when we were discussing anchoring in deserts under trample-burrs; also, when we were discussing hydrochory and the danger of dispersal by wind to unsuitable habitats in the case of orchids (p. 53). I pointed (1957 b) to the same danger for *Sonneratia*, brought as an immigrant by sea currents to Riu Kiu but doomed to sterility there by lack of pollinating bats. Further synecological research might show more cases of harm by dispersal outside the natural community. The rain forest will also demonstrate this (see p. 86).

The more limited the suitable habitat, the greater the waste. *Epilobium angustifolium* is limited in this way to newly opened-up spots in forests and residential areas. Thanks to the "waste" in anemochory it appears immediately, like a microbe on its substrate. Only incidentally, when no climax-forms can suppress it, this species persists by means of its rhizome.

There exists, however, a different strategy, the limitation of dispersal to the already occupied, obviously suitable spot. This is defensive strategy, avoiding useless waste in the wide desert.

The Israeli botanist ZOHARY mentioned in his book "Plant Life of Palestine" (1962) ten types of atelechory: baryspermy (our barochory), carpospermy (monospermy without dispersal), synaptospermy, myxospermy, trypanocarpy (boring diaspores), hygrochasy, basicarpy, heterocarpy, amphicarpy, and geocarpy. We shall discuss some of these categories separately and add to his trypanocarpy and myxospermy the other anchoring devices.

2. Synaptospermy

MURBECK (1920) described the keeping or even bringing together of many seeds until germination as synaptospermy, or a limitation of separation. The phenomenon was found convergently in plants of arid North-African regions in 140 cases (mostly annuals), in contrast to 5 in Scandinavia.

The simplest case is non-dehiscence of many-seeded fruits, but in others, as species of *Beta*, *Spinacia* and *Forskahlea*, the spiny or woolly fruits of the entire inflorescence stick together.

MURBECK admits the general disadvantage of many seedlings staying together but thinks that this is less important in open vegetations. He states as the main local functional significance, confirmed by actual observations, that extra-envelopment offers better protection in the long, dry period; furthermore, the complex prevents too rapid drying out during the all-important germination period, and, last but not least, the tissues of the complex can, during germination, hold more absorbed rainwater than isolated seeds can. He admits that the matter has other, accessory aspects, viz. better anchoring of the whole in the sand as a brake, (the diaspores are often spiny) and a special dispersability by the spines, though synaptospermy as such is not considered as designed for dispersal.

Having observed that in *Beta* and similar forms the complexes are tumblers which catch more wind than single diaspores, and being also aware of the fact that so many cases mentioned have trample-burrs and adhesive burrs, I think that MURBECK neglected the dispersal effect somewhat. The detachment of the whole complex also belongs to the syndrome of these diaspores. This aspect may very well have been another background. The cited cases of synaptospermy in *Prosopis* and *Zizyphus* point to dispersal by ruminants. The germinating together may also have a relation with stimulative physiology and with the breeding system, with incompatibility, and little mobility or paucity of pollinators. This deserves investigation.

We know of no work on atelechory in other continents, but ZOHARY (1937) investigated the phenomenon for Palestine. He found it in 243 species, spread over many families and then in special sub-groups. Instances are desert-grasses (some spp. of *Aegilops, Triticum, Pennisetum*), Leguminosae (pods of *Medicago, Astragalus*, pods and heads of *Trifolium*), Composite heads, indehiscent Cruciferae (especially Brassicae), fruit-calyces of some Labiatae. He admits that synaptospermy is not *in toto* simply atelechorous. In Compositae, it leads to the disappearance of pappus and in many other cases to monospermy of the fruit proper, as in the burrs of the Crucifer *Clypeola*, the spikelets of *Aegilops* and the legumes of *Trifolium*. In consideration of the origin of Compositae and Gramineae and their fruits, this aspect cannot be neglected.

3. Basicarpy

The formation of fruits immediately above ground level is seen in many plants from semi-deserts. The older authors called it hypogeocarpy, but MURBECK introduced the newer term as part of the atelechorous syndrome, as its protective aspect.

STOPP (1958 b) called attention to basicarpy in the South-African desert flora, describing grasses (species of *Enneapogon, Cleistogenes, Stipa*, etc.) with partly aerial, partly basicarpous spikelets, the latter bradysporous and heavily protected during the rainless period. His inclusion of *Elephan-torhiza burchelli* (Leguminosae) among the basicarpous plants requires further investigation.

Basicarpy as a mere phenomenon occurs elsewhere and may have a function totally different from waiting in a protected position, as in deserts. It occurs in Zingiberaceae in rain forests and may there functionally belong to the field of pollination. We already discussed basicaulicarpy in the part on reptile-dispersal.

4. Geocarpy

The burying near the motherplant of all diaspores (geocarpy) or of a part of them (amphicarpy) is a very effective method of ensuring atelechory. In the older literature, where only distant dispersal was considered impor-tant, geocarpy was thought to be functional only as a protective device, directed especially against grazing animals. However, it is immediately clear that it can keep desert plants (mostly annuals that have to grow from seed year after year) in the right spot in an inhospitable environment.

For Palestine, a dry country, ZOHARY (1937) listed many species (mainly Papilionaceae) with amphicarpy. In the whole world, about 30 species are known with this character, a phenomenon still in development, and furthered by diverse means, in various families. Amphicarpy is often subject to pheno-typic variation. It has some connection with floral cleistogamy, a connection absent in full geocarpy. ULBRICH (1928) discusses many cases, mainly European species of *Viola, Vicia* and *Lathyrus,* of the latter two concerning species growing in arid regions. For America *Ranunculus hilairea* (Andine dry regions), *Cardamine chenopodiifolia* (Argentine and Brazil). I must remark that the North-American plant *Amphicarpa bracteata* (the hog-peanut) does not grow in an arid environment; the deviating, buried pods are transported and cached by squirrels. The vernacular name is due to the fact that hogs also dig them up. Included are some grasses, even perennials, and some species of *Commelina* from South-Asia, not desert plants.

Full geocarpy is rarely found in fruits produced from flowers that were already underground. However, it does occur in this way in some Palestine Araceae such as *Stylochiton and Biarum.* Lists of geocarps by older authors do not always differentiate between geocarpy, amphicarpy, and basicarpy — and between the different ecological classes to which the respective cases belong, as illustrated below.

For Palestine, ZOHARY described 5 cases (there are 16 in the world); his description includes their physiology. Involved are some Papilionaceae, but also a *Callitriche* found in temporary pools. The number of seeds in the fruits or the number of flowers in the heads is reduced, and dehiscence fails. The best known cases are some Papilionaceae such as *Arachis hypogea* (from

Brazil), *Voandzeia subterranea* (West Africa), *Astragalus hypogaeus* (West Siberia), some Cruciferae, and *Geococcus pusillus* from Australian deserts.

To consider geocarpy only in relation to atelochory in deserts is again simplistic. The subterranean clover *(Trifolium subterraneum)* occurs also in France and Britain. It even has strong colonizing tendencies, as became evident in Australia (MORLEY in BAKER and STEBBINS, 1965). Some of the fruits are dispersed as burrs and rollers; also, as in other species of *Trifolium*, achenes are eaten and dispersed internally by grazing animals. That the species is favoured in a community by grazing may even be due to the ancient aspect of protection of the buried part of the fruits. In the Orient, some related species with less well-developed geocarpy occur.

Though there is a marked preponderance in arid regions, the phenomenon of geocarpy (as demonstrated already for amphicarpy) occurs also in moist habitats, which points to a different function there. South-African *Falkia repens* (Convolvulaceae) grows along water (cf. also *Voandzeia*).

The phenomenon also occurs in rainy tropical regions. The African rain forest has a *Begonia hypogaea*, growing near creeks and producing berries. In geocarpous species of *Ficus*, the phenomenon has an entirely different background (see p. 23). The case of *Cucumis humifructus* has, although the plant lives in deserts, a connection with dispersal by digging animals that live underground (see p. 46).

A curious case is the one reported to me by Dr. H. C. D. DE WIT (Wageningen). *Cephaelis densinerva* (Rubiaceae) is a tall shrub growing on the margin of forests in Cameroon. The stalk of the inflorescence, in its upper part, grows down to the ground as a rope up to 4 meters in length. It is there among the debris that the small flowers open and the berries develop later on. It has yet to be determined what this signifies, either for the flowers or the fruits.

The simple inclusion, in lists of geocarpous plants, of myrmecochores with fruit stalks that bend down or even considering such presentation to soil- or ground animals as "pseudo-geocarpy" (ULBRICH for *Cyclamen*), means increase of confusion. In the amphicarpous species of *Viola* (*V. hirta*, *V. odorata*) the "geocarpy" is clearly a further extension of such presentation. They are myrmecochores from a moist habitat.

B. Polychory and Attendant Phenomena

1. General

In the foregoing sub-chapters we have met many cases where diaspores are dispersed by more than one agent. This is designated as diplochory or even polychory, in contrast to the normal case of haplochory. Sometimes the "legitimate" way, as indicated by the condition of relatives and by remnants of adaptive structures, seems superseded by utilization and new development of some other character, which may originally have been incidental.

In this chapter, we shall see that often consideration under one heading or caption is unrealistic. A special character, then, proves important not only because it is directed towards two agents but also because it is connected with something that lies outside the sphere of mere dispersal. It then possesses two aspects relevant to two different fields of life. One aspect may be connected with the phenomenon of establishment, occurring later. Here, our classification by agents seems simplistic and invites replacement by one according to the destination of the diaspore. This would fit the later habitat of the plant. In many desert plants, the hard burrs that are observed so frequently show the apparently contradictory aspects of being dispersed and being anchored. In some shore-plants (*Cocos* c. s.), we find two aspects to be considered: dispersal and arrival on a dry shore. In the cases of *Spinifex* and *Agropyron*, described in this book, the diplochory is of vital importance. The combination again means a refinement, directed dispersal, somewhat along the lines followed in flower-pollination. For shore-and desert-plants we shall discuss this cooperation in regard to the habitat under the heading of establishment. We do this, in part, to justify our hold on this field.

Self-anchoring water-burrs or seeds with flotation-slime may stick to birds' feet. On the other hand, real burrs of *Xanthium* may actually be water-dispersed to river-banks. In some regions the bradysporous berries of *Hippophae rhamnoides* are not eaten by birds, but shrivel and drift about over ground, snow and water, propelled by the wind (MÜLLER-SCHNEIDER, 1955). Berries in transition towards myrmecochory *(Trillium)* may profit from two agents with different, complementary functions, as is the case in many other myrmecochores. The anemochorous fruits of *Acer* were found in caches of rodents, where they germinated. *Alnus* and *Aster tripolium* are anemochorous as well as hydrochorous. In cases of diplochory, different races may express different preferences. Sometimes the combined structural possibilities, together with a broad vegetative tolerance, lead to two different possible habitats. *Ximenia americana* is sometimes found as a seashore plant (due to flotation of the kernel), sometimes as an inland plant (due to pigeon-dispersal of the drupes). *Mimosa asperata* is found in Java on river shores as well as on dry fields along animal trails, due respectively to the floating of the seeds and to their spiny joints. Such cases demonstrate the influence of dispersal on distribution and speciation.

In 1957 b I described quite a number of plant species that entertain connections with both bats and the sea; *Cycas rumphii, Calophyllum ino-phyllum, Hernandia peltata, Terminalia catappa, Inocarpus edulis,* and species of *Pandanus.* The bond with the sea is the secondary one, although it is important for distant dispersal and colonization; the one with bats takes care of inland settlement. *Afzelia bijuga, Hippomane mancinella* and *Phoenix palustris* and others might be added. In these plants the two-fold dispersal has a curious synecological aspect. Sea-currents bring them to the shore of islands, but bats and birds that can live on the fruits transport them inland. This provides an answer to the sophistic question: which came first, fruit-bats without fruits or bat-fruits without bats?

The synergy between the anemochory and synzoochory of *Pinus* and the dispersal of *Quercus* was discussed on p. 27.

Some authors speak of collateral zoochory or anemochory. A wealth of terms may be coined in this field by lovers of term-manufacture.

2. Heterocarpy

Polychory does not always repose on the described characters in one and the same diaspore (isocarpy). The plant may avoid putting all its eggs in one basket in other ways. One method consists in differentiation in structure of its diaspores, another one in differentiation as to time of presentation and/or germination. The first method may lead to amphicarpy, a situation where both aerial and subterranean fruits are produced. This differentiation leads to the development of one kind of diaspore for dispersal and another for defensive non-dispersal, as mentioned under atelochory.

Another differentiation produces ordinary heterodiaspory (heterocarpy and heterospermy) with both kinds of diaspores functioning in dispersal, albeit dispersal by different methods; one of these mostly serves for limited, synaptospermous dispersal. This is also the most frequent method in plants from arid zones, where a reserve is kept to bridge an unfavourable period. The phenomenon is found in Gramineae and Compositae, the specialists in dispersal refinement. *Aegilops* has one-seeded and more compound diaspores (ZOHARY, 1937); other grasses are discussed on p. 78.

In the Compositae, heterocarpy was investigated by BECKER (1913). There is an apparent basis for its development in the difference between outer and inner flowers in the capitulum, but ZOHARY (1950) showed that the differentiation in fruits was often of independent origin, especially arising in Liguliflorae, etc. withouth differentiation in flowers (cf. BURTT on p. 15). The general impression is that the outer fruits in those cases tend to be without dispersal-structures and stay in the involucrum the longest, while the inner ones are built for earlier, faster and farther dispersal, being provided with pappus, wings and hooks. So it is in the American genera *Ximesia, Guttierresia* and *Synedrella*, and also in the Mediterranean form *Hedypnois cretica*. The well-known *Calendula* even has three kinds.

Xanthium and other genera show, next to a slight morphological difference of no direct chorological consequence, a difference in the time of germination between the only two fruits contained in the detached capitulum. This leads to a differentiation that will be discussed later. BECKER already showed that in this and other cases the difference in germination is due to the difference in pericarps, so that the plants have no heterospermy proper.

For Palestine, ZOHARY (1937) has given a list of 100 cases (all annuals but including families other than the Compositae) where the retarded diaspores provide atelochory. Cruciferae *(Heterocarpus)* and Leguminosae *(Desmodium heterocarpum)* join in. In some *Rumex* species basal and higher-placed fruits differ in form. Here, germination in the two types is about the same, but the seedlings differ in size (HARPER in BAKER and STEBBINS, 1965). The strongest heterocarpy exists in the Mediterranean species *Fedia cornucopiae* (Valerianaceae) which has three astonishingly different kinds of fruits, with anemochorous, epizoochorous, hydrochorous, and myrmecochorous properties. LEVINA (1966) published (in Russian) a review of many papers on the subject that thave been published in Russia.

ZOHARY (1937) lists cases in Palestine of a different phenomenon, heteromericarpy, where the two parts of one fruit are different in form and function, one part being atelochorous in most cases; *Cakile* and *Rapistrum* are well known in this regard.

A third term, heterospermy, is applied to differentiate between the seeds themselves, a phenomenon known of old in *Spergularia marginata* and Chenopodiaceae. ZOHARY investigated this also for Leguminosae with seeds diverging in time and power of swelling, spread over some years. HARPER (in BAKER and STEBBINS, 1965) reported on heterospermy in weeds with (I fear) an agriculturist's disregard for the differences between seeds and fruits. In *Chenopodium album,* four types are borne on one plant, their difference in germination assisting the species in aggressivity. Purely physiological heterodiaspory (the heteroblasty of EVENARI), connected with differences in situation on the plant, may be frequent.

2. Tachyspory

The foregoing cases lead up to the mentioned differentiation with time among diaspores; differences become manifest in time of presentation, dispersal and also germination, a field not within the area of dispersal proper but not separable from it in practice.

For our purposes, it is necessary to refer to some classical terms. SERNANDER distinguished tachysporous plants (tachy = fast), where the diaspores are set free immediately after maturation, and bradysporous plants (brady = slow) where liberation comes only after a long delay. The delay can be one winter ("Wintersteher") or one summer, or some indefinite period (macrobiocarpy) as in spp. of *Pinus, Callistemon* and many Proteaceae (see

p. 100). The most extreme cases of macrobiocarpy are found in a ragweed *(Ambrosia bryantii)*, where the thorny involucrum remains imbedded in the plant for some seasons, and in *Pinus attenuata* where the cones stay on the plants and are overgrown by the bark, so that their seeds come free only at the death of the tree.

In periodically dry regions the timing is often provided by xerochastic opening of the containers (in anemochores and ballists) or by hygrochastic opening when humidity is the necessary signal. The fruiting calyces of Labiatae, the study of which by STOPP should be followed up, vary strongly in this respect; they are important organs in dispersal. Many desert plants with heteromericarpy have, in one and the same fruit, bradysporous and tachysporous parts. ZOHARY (1937) analyzed this for Palestine, STOPP (1962) for some Pedaliaceae in Angola. Many desert Mesembryanthemaceae strew seeds only when rain comes (hygrochasy) with ensuing weak ombrohydrochory. They retain part of the seeds in special pockets to serve in later, distant dispersal (SCHWANTES, 1952, and IHLENFELDT, 1959).

C. Concluding Remarks on Synecology

1. Deserts

We have seen on several occasions that the influence of dispersal reaches farther than the individual plant species and can characterize communities. This became especially clear in semi-desert areas, on which we already possess the extensive book by H. WALTER, "Die Vegetation der Erde in ökologischer Betrachtung, I". In this book, however, pollination, dispersal and germination are strongly under-represented when compared to vegetative physiology. More ecological minds have presented us with details concerning the reproductive processes in addition to vegetative details such as geophyty, prostrate growth-form, etc.

To recapitulate some data from the foregoing parts: MURBECK found synaptospermy in 140 species of the arid North African flora, with 100 reaching into the Sahara. ZOHARY found the flora in Palestine to be 11 % synaptospermous; this against the $2^1/2$ % in southern France reported by MÜLLER-SCHNEIDER and almost 0 % in Fenno-Scandia. MURBECK found myxospermy in North Africa in 11 % of the species, in true desert regions even in 20 %, but in Scandinavia only in 3 %. In considering such regions with their atelochory, one gets an impression of dispersal totally different from the one conveyed by textbooks that are based on the model of Western Europe. Our current views on Cruciferous and Leguminous fruits should also be radically revised for these regions, even to the extent of shedding new light on possible evolutionary processes in ovaries and fruits in general (see p. 121).

A percentual review of dispersal-agents involved would be equally interesting, considering the many tumbleweeds, trample-burrs, etc.

Anchoring is achieved not only by the devices described for desert-dia-spores but also by depressions in the soil, that are, moreover, slightly damper. Footprints of camels often show massing of seedlings.

Though the foregoing concerns mostly annuals, whereas American writers paid more attention to shrubs and trees, it remains remarkable that, in a special paper on the subject (SPALDING, 1909) and in later monographs on North-American deserts, we find no mention of the above-described characteristics except for the frequency of burrs. Some herbs are tumble-weeds *(Atriplex canescens)*. These desert-like regions also deviate from African counterparts in the matter of pollination (little myophily). Some anchoring in depressions and by shrubs is described, not achieved by special devices on diaspores. Contrary to atelochory, obligatory distantiation of new plants is described for some species of *Cotinus, Cercidium* and *Olneya*. This is achieved by germination of the seed only after it has undergone abrasion by drifting over the surface for some distance. Some timing of presentation by means of hygrochasy has been described, e. g. for the pods of *Acacia constricta*.

2. The Rain Forest

Our views on fruits and their evolution have also been changed greatly by considering tropical conditions, even though in recent years the im-pression has been created that dispersal and its organs are of no importance there, at least in the rain forest. (For the tropical seashore vegetation the great influence of dispersal is readily recognized.) Therefore we shall now turn our attention to reproduction in the rain forest as a community. It is at the same time archaic and complex, stable and polymorphic. It is a strongly homeostatic unity, full of feedback, and thus with a stable inner life governed by many influences. Its floristic complexity means there is a certain distance between conspecific trees, producing an independence from "pest-pressure", as already indicated by RIDLEY (p. 107). It does not show exclusion of vicariant species, though this circumstance does not justify the opinion that the struggle for life and interspecific natural selection are absent.

The complexity also provides flowers and fruits all the year round, quite a different situation from the condition in temperate forests, where fruit-eaters cannot (or not always) find food and where the herbaceous undergrowth has to offer some relief early in the season. We saw that even in vegetations of shrubs and herbs there, the continuity of food is not guaranteed and that fruit-eaters can only temporarily subsist on their usual diet, switching (when necessary) to animal food or to dry fruits, the latter also fit for storage during the unfavourable period. Vertebrates subsisting on flowers are excluded unless they can migrate to the subtropics, which in Europe is difficult.

In the rain-forest, each plant species makes reproduction by means of resident animals possible for another species that flowers and fruits later on; this is true even if the later one is a congeneric species with competitive vegetative requirements. A similar situation exists with regard to pollinators. In this field, not only highly developed specialists should be considered as permanently present and bound to the forests as a whole. Archaic pollinators, such as beetles and flies, also show this bond, and even more obviously, since they and their larvae (not being specialized for flowers) have to subsist on the living or decaying material of plants and animals in the whole community.

The poorly developed dispersal potential of trees makes for a sufficiently uniform distribution within the rain forest and also for recolonization of adjacent "wound areas" (secondary vegetations in large gaps). The largeness of, and lack of dormancy in, seeds is connected not only with the special dispersers, but also with a special way of rejuvenation, viz. by the omni-presence of waiting seedlings in the small gaps mentioned before.

We may justifiably be curious about the fate of reforestation experiments that start with the adult organization of climax trees and with pure stands. One might extrapolate the concept of homeostasis and closedness into the vegetative sphere, considering also the plant nutrients. This would, of course, not imply that in the vegetative sphere the environment has no influence at all. There may exist local variations in composition due to edaphic influences (though this is not a dominating factor). Under marginal edaphic conditions (as in the mangrove) a special selection of climax forms or pioneers may be evident, resembling temperate "associations". Here one factor dominates.

I could illustrate the principle of "ecological parasitism" on the complex with the example of orchids utilizing pre-existent ecological niches, food, substrate and pollinators, but this is not the occasion (see under v. d. PIJL and DODSON, 1967).

RICHARDS (1952) could maintain the concept of uniformity in the optimal rain forest because he neglected the biotic element and reproduction. Temperate sociologists were glad to find, beside the mentioned marginal "associations" in very poor conditions, some connections with their familiar concepts when they discovered "aggregates" of one dominant in some rain forests. These may, however, often be due to the fact that just one species was in fruit near an incidental gap, or had seedlings ready in it. According to JONES (1955) the aggregates contain young trees and are less obvious in regard to emergents.

In the following Table 1, I compare the climax forest with its predecessor after large-scale catastrophes, the secondary forest. For a characterization of the latter see RICHARDS (1952, p. 377—386). It shows some characteristics of the temperate forests, which are still more impoverished in species and especially in pollinators and dispersers. I must leave the zoological side to other ecologists. The table may seem somewhat superfluous here, but it can serve other purposes. The points pertaining to germination and rejuvenation will be discussed in a following chapter. In this regard we shall also find differences between the rain-forest and the nomadic pioneer vegetation of the secondary forest. Curiously, the only tree-like Composite in South-Asian rain forests, *Vernonia arborea*, does not belong to the true pioneers, though it still has rather small, pappose fruits. It settled late on Krakatau in existing woodland: in light rain forest it rejuvenates itself. Therefore it seems a succesful intruder, not a form regularly killed by climax forms. Its height (up to 25 m) surpasses that of the famous Composite trees of St. Helena and the Galapagos islands. Other woody species of *Vernonia* are mentioned for secondary forest in Nigeria.

Table 1

Secondary Forest	Climax Rain Forest
total, new colonization from reservist-seeds after destruction	permanent growth, local rejuvenation in gaps
germination in light	germination in shadow
strong dormancy	weak dormancy
seeds small	seeds often large
immediate outgrowth of seedlings	seedlings waiting for a chance
rapid and distant dispersal, much anemochory, many dry fruits	limited dispersal, much endozoochory, many large, fleshy fruits
no internal rejuvenation, life-span limited by overgrowing	constant rejuvenation, life-span unlimited, layers and shade-tolerance change
very open to outside influences, more mixed and migrant visitors	closed-off inner reproductive system, constant food production for pollinators and dispersers
pollinators less dependent on living whole, specialized	many archaic flowers for beetles and flies bound to whole for life-cycle
unstable, more open to pests	homeostatic, more immune to pests

After this digression on inner coherence, we go back to simple characterization of the community from the viewpoint of dispersal. Perhaps the first published estimate in the direction of a dispersal-spectrum was the one by STAPF in 1894 on the forest of Mt. Kinabalu (Borneo): 35—40 % fleshy fruits, 25—28 % wind-dispersed, the rest unspecialized. The spectrum can, however, as STAPF showed, vary at different altitudes due to the influence of wind which increases with altitude. In the different layers of vegetation it can also vary, but a large percentage has no special means of dispersal. RICHARDS (1952) pointed to the wind dispersal of some top-story trees.

The rain forest of South Nigeria has, according to JONES (1956), in the emergents 46 % of the species wind-dispersed and 46 % animal-dispersed, but in the lower stories this is 7 % and 71 % respectively. KEAY (1957) found there in an old secondary forest the following shares of wind-dispersed species: in emergent trees 56 %, upper-stratum lianas 48 %, upper-stratum trees 25 %, lower-stratum trees 2 %, shrubs, treelets and lower lianas nil. Herbs and epiphytes were not considered. All cauliforous plants produce fleshy fruits.

Later on, a finer differentiation will become necessary, a. o. between small- and large-seeded fleshy fruits, the first being more typical for bird-dispersed pioneers.

3. Epiphytes

In this component of the rain forest and other communities the transport factor plays a more dominant role, since the substrate requires special devices for arrival and settlement of diaspores.

In many instances (in open forests) we find simple anemochory with dust-like diaspores and plumes, often a transition from anemochory with some modification for attachment to the bark of trees. Many epiphytes, such as those in the large genus *Ficus,* have small, bird- or bat-dispersed seeds sticking on the substratum with the excreta; rarely *(Peperomia)* viscid, epizoochorous diaspores.

Even some epiphytic orchids *(Aerides, Jonopsis)* possess hooks on the seeds.

The group of ant-epiphytes was discussed under ants as agents.

The absence of epiphytes among Leguminosae (in contrast to its many climbers) may be based partly on the seed-character of the family, partly on its lack of perennating vegetative organs, another point of importance for life as an epiphyte.

HEINTZE (1932) filled the two instalments of his book with data on European occasional epiphytes (tycho-epiphytes) and how they arrived in the crown of pollard-willows, etc.

4. Island Floras

Although the analysis of further regional floras lies outside the scope of our book, we may make an exception for small, strongly isolated regions. There, one can study the transport factor intensively, and also the influence of long isolation of a new community on speciation; and, finally, the fitting together of immigrants in a new synecological whole.

The first instance of such an "insular" community is the one of far-disjunct mountain tops. STAPF (1894) already pointed to the apparent lack of specialized dispersal mechanisms in the alpine region of Mt. Kinabalu (Borneo). For the Malaysian mountain flora as a whole, VAN STEENIS (1933/36) analyzed all factors possibly responsible for the distribution of the non-tropical species. From the geological and historical factors that had to be considered, he excluded a profound influence of the ice-age. He also excluded the factor of dispersal, on the basis of present-day data on dispersal. The isolated habitats of *Primula prolifera* (without apparent means of distant dispersal) are presented as illustrative and also the occurrence of some summit plants with berries on a few mountain-tops only (obviously denying local effects on ecesis). He doubted any effect of occasional events, such as cyclones. As we saw before, the riddle of the distribution thus remains unsolved in a causal sense.

I note that zoologists found in isolated islands or on mountain tops that the impoverished habitats may inhibit coexistence of species living together elsewhere. Incidental first arrivals or last remainers may exclude competing species of birds by lack of niche diversity. This circumstance may also influence plant distribution on mountain tops.

In a recent symposium (CONSTANCE, 1963) on long-distance dispersal between North and South America of the many West-American disjuncts, attention was paid to migrating birds as vectors. Proof remained vague. For a subsequent analysis see CRUDEN (1966). Stepwise dispersal ("moun-tain-hopping") was proposed. Such theories do not, in my opinion, take into account the necessity of intermediary, local establishment and of local pollinators and dispersers. The same is true for "island-hopping" in the following part — on real islands.

The famous instance of the continental island of Krakatau and its new vegetation, though remaining of considerable interest, is of limited impor-tance in the consideration of trans-oceanic transport. Its recolonization was, moreover, largely a matter of increasing possibility of establishment on the substrate. In the beginning many more plants were transported over the short distance than became established. Even diaspores of inland plants were transported to the new beach and lived there for a time.

The old story of recapitulation of evolution in the changing vegetation cannot be maintained as generally valid. For details of the succession and the transport see ERNST (1934) and DOCTERS VAN LEEUWEN (1936). Sea transport was quickly saturated, soon leading to normal shore composition. Overseas transport by wind and birds respectively followed, in that order. The diplochory of the plants mentioned on p. 81 (with dispersal by bats and sea currents) was helpful in establishing a community.

With regard to truly oceanic islands, opinions differ strongly on the possibility of long-distance dispersal: the discussion has become muddy by the introduction of moot points concerning ancient land bridges, ancient continental boundaries, continental drift, etc. I pass over violent old disputes on this question, such as those between GULICK and SKOTTSBERG. RIDLEY (pp. 674—690) tended to accept long-distance dispersal by birds and drifting logs, giving many cited cases as proof (pp. 25, 29). To mention a new instance: TAYLOR (1954) found on Macquarie Island, 950 km southwest of New Zealand, 35 species of vascular plants. It was once completely covered by ice and was never connected with larger land masses by bridges. The plants may all have arrived fairly recently with the aid of birds, by means of hooks and viscid berries. He reported such diaspores as actually being found on albatrosses. Endemism is practically absent.

FOSBERG (1948, 1951, 1963) has always been a protagonist of dispersal to oceanic Pacific Islands by means of sea currents, jet streams and sea birds. He attempted to determine the number of successful colonizations needed to account for their present flora. Of 1729 species of seed plants on certain islands, only 272 represent more or less the original immigrants. For their establishment, only one successful colonization every 25,000 years was necessary. Moreover, the disharmonic floral compositon, which differs from island to island, is considered to be proof in itself. For Hawaii he postulated 69 species as a basis of development; of these, 21 remained in the original state, the other 48 giving rise to the remainder of the flora through later evolution. This now-deviating component may even be partly derived from drift plants which originally possessed large seeds.

GUPPY (1906) had already pointed to the increase in seed size after immigration on islands, and CARLQUIST (1966 a, b) further developed this topic. After studying the means of transport, he defended long-distance dispersal as basic for Hawaii, also the evolutionary developments following immigration. The latter resulted in a low dispersal rate in a stable vegetation. This represents not just the adjustment to "wind pressure", presumed for flightless island insects. The process of "precinctiveness" was made evident for some Compositae in Pacific islands of overwhelmingly American affinity. Seed size increased, sometimes resulting in gigantism, (Stenogyne, Tetraplasandra); the hooks of Bidens decreased in size or disappeared. In the Galapagos Islands, the composite genus Lecocarpus acquired, as a secondary mechanism, a wing-like bract on a pappusless achene. The general lack of dispersibility is thus demonstrated as a secondary phenomenon.

An interesting discussion between scientists on either side of the question is found in the symposium proceedings edited by GRESSITT (1963). Here, VAN STEENIS defended the concept of land bridges against FOSBERG, maintaining the idea of endemics as relicts. Beside the general fact that plants with and without evident dispersal mechanisms may occupy comparable areas, his main argument was that tropical lowland seeds are too large for distant dispersal and that disharmony in island floras is not more pronounced than in comparable, isolated continental regions. Both authors take as a main basis the "steady state", the permanence of geographic and climatic conditions during the evolution of higher flowering plants in and after the Cretaceous. Continental drift is excluded as being already past its prime.

For a more extended review of VAN STEENIS' views opposing trans-oceanic dispersal, see his special article defending ancient land-bridges (1962). The paper is, admittedly, somewhat negativistic in its defence. It cuts in regard to lack of pappus of Compositae and to largeness of many insular diaspores the possibility of gigantism, precinctiveness and of derivation from large drift-seeds. In regard to the impossibility of spread and establishment of rain-forest plants outside their forests, it neglects the fact that they can follow pioneering nomads (c. f. *Durio* and *Vernonia arborea*). VAN STEENIS mentions *Gahnia*, *Carex*, etc. as spread over immense areas, yet having no structures for endozoic or epizoic dispersal by birds. Against the failures of establishment of sown seeds he mentions, stand, however, all adventives that did succeed.

A general curiosity in the "tracks" of many distributionists is that these scientists use tracks as the reflection of dynamic, progressive extension, but switch to a static concept of relict-nature as soon as small, disjunct areas are to be considered. When disjuncts are found far from a common centre of origin and without obvious means of dispersal one asks how they first arrived and looks for a condition changed in some respect.

Further concepts related to ancient land-bridges lie too far outside our field to be dealt with here. Antarctica, Pacifica, Gondwana may be left to distributionists.

5. Plant Sociology and Dispersal

When dealing with new and rejuvenating vegetation, the student of communities cannot afford to neglect the transport factor. The creation of dunes in Holland is based on the special dispersal methods of *Triticum (Agropyron) junceum*. After primary wind transport overland to the sea, the fruits can (at least locally) endure further transport by salt water. They are washed ashore and germinate in flood marks rich in debris; they do not die off after a year like *Salsola* and *Cakile* but remain rooted in the rich substrate. Then, dunes form around them (VAN DIEREN, 1934).

FEEKES (1936) studied the succession in a new polder in the Netherlands, stressing for the initial phase (occurring in the region still covered with salty water) the importance of "drift", plant-complexes carrying also non-halophilous diaspores, so that the later-appearing soil was by no means virginal. In the following more or less dry phase the contribution of epizoochory and endozoochory by water-fowl was important. Many migrating thrushes and finches later contributed, after feeding on *Atriplex* and *Suaeda*.

Endozoochory of real berries played only a small role in this wet, semi-halophilous phase, in an ill-fitting biotope. His results relating to anemo-chory have been discussed before.

The American school of "ecologists" (mostly sociologists) was always dynamic, paying much attention to succession and showing some interest in dispersal; as described here, European plant sociologists as a group, however, have seriously neglected the transport factor. Their synecology is mainly descriptive, and so are their succession studies. FEEKES apologized that the succession in the polder is not a proper object for theoretical sociological considerations but tried to apply them nevertheless.

The study of agricultural weed communities also offers such difficulties, since they are rather incidental, ever-changing complexes, associations in the literal sense. In a sociological symposium on anthropogenous vegetations (TÜXEN, 1966) all reproductive processes, so crucial in this matter, remained undiscussed.

The more experimental researchers in Europe (cf. KNOPP, 1954) paid special attention to measurable factors acting in the vegetative sphere. In the reproductive sphere they limited their attention, probably rightly, to ger-mination. Perhaps dispersal seems to them too clearly a property of the individual species, though important in succession. HEIMANS (1954) tried for years to arouse interest in the transport factor, coining on the side of the habitat the concept of accessibility, which had already been applied in historical plant geography. Its counterpart in plants might be considered too, under the name of "agressivity". This characteristic has been analyzed for weeds, as discussed in chapter X.

For some large-scale, physiognomic communities such as deserts and rain-forests, dispersal spectra have already been described in the foregoing parts. As my knowledge of "plant sociology" is restricted, I refer readers for the study of dispersal in diverse associations to the discussion of some European papers in pp. 129—132 of MÜLLER-SCHNEIDER (1955). There graphic representation of dispersal-classes in associations is to be found.

The main part of MOLINIER-MÜLLER's study (1938) on the different communities of southern France consists of a comparison between their dispersal spectra, also between the succession stages. Clear differences were found and the connection between aridity and autochory was confirmed.

SALISBURY (1942) plotted fruit setting, seed size and output, and the viability of diaspores against habitat conditions, finding interesting correla-tions to be discussed elsewhere. DANSEREAU and LEMS (1957) felt that a functional analysis of sociological units and succession should also involve coefficients of dispersal types. They tested this on North American plant communities. The results were similar to those of MOLINIER-MÜLLER. They mixed agents of dispersal, agents of break-off and presumed morphological adaptations in the naming of types, sometimes deliberately ignoring the fact that a winged diaspore is not necessarily anemochorous. DANSEREAU and LEMS, on this basis, proposed the new grouping of diaspores, mentioned here on p. 8. The readily recognizable morphological features were taken as criteria for constructing what they call dispersal spectra in communities. I admit that this procedure is probably justified in their field. I criticize their terminology and its application (by others) in our field, the ecology of dispersal as a general process.

6. Coordinated Dispersal

We found some traits of coordination in the rain forest, more than in other vegetations, where (at best) parallelism was encountered. In the chapter on weeds we shall find an equalization in dispersal with crop-plants, leading to coordination, by human agency. It is worth investigating whether in higher plants something on the lines of lichens exists, where the components can spread together.

The diplochory of some tropical shore plants (see p. 81) does not only provide additional dispersal inland but also makes life possible for bats and birds. When migrating, these can at the same time bring in other inland plants.

More evidence in this direction is to be expected in parasitic plants, where we found some precision, e. g. in the burying of seeds by ants (*Lathraea, Mystropetalon*), in hyperparasitic Loranthaceae reaching their host plant by means of the common disperser *(Dicaeum)*. ATSATT (1965) reported coordinated dispersal of the parasite *Orthocarpus* as the diaspores hook in on the pappus fruit of the host *(Hypochoeris)*. The combination with an introduced host seems accidental, but is fully effective. If one wishes to see the plants in "ant-gardens" as an association, one finds coordination in dispersal in a community. Perhaps even in other ant-plants.

FEEKES (1936) pointed out that tumbleweeds can carry in their complexes many diaspores of other plants from the community, even rather heavy ones.

VII. Establishment

A. General

Treating only the transport of diaspores in this book, would result in a picture without background, not fully deserving the name of ecology. This has already become clear in the earlier chapters, where a discussion of the nature of diaspores showed, time and again, bonds with later phases of life. A similar situation was found in the time of presentation.

We have to deal here also with the aspect of germination of the diaspores just as one has to in floral ecology where processes, starting to work after the transport of microspores, are found to have been "built-in" from the very beginning in the properties of spore and stigma. They have to be put into our picture, the more so because many aspects are neglected in laboratory work on germination. One might say for many diaspores that the destination is built-in. Admittedly, diaspore dispersal never attains the exactness which pollination displays in reaching with precision a favourable substrate at the right time; still, we may draw parallels with the matter treated in "The principles of pollination-ecology" (FAEGRI and VAN DER PIJL, 1966). The peaks are myrmecochory, Loranthaceae and Dicaeum, and some mechanisms of atelochory centered already around germination in a favourable place.

We have already seen that some discussions of recolonization (e. g., those concerning Krakatau) neglected the suitability of the substrate. On the other hand, many other studies concerned with recolonization after volcanic activity paid attention almost exclusively to succession in connection with the changing substrate and neglected dispersal.

On the side of diaspores, the chain to success is the following: maturation (+ dormancy) → presentation → dispersal (+ afterripening + protection + longevity) → fixation → germination (+ breaking of dormancy) → establishment (ecesis of CLEMENTS, in a certain sense).

It should be noted that this refers to the plant individual. In regard to a plant species, we may speak of establishment only when the individual reproduces itself.

B. Fixation

In anemochores, hairs may finally act as anchors on the substrate (they can easily be transformed into them entirely). We saw this in plumose epiphytes. In desert plants and water plants, the dispersal and fixation-functions of burrs are concurrent. The anchoring aspect in desert plants is clear in their myxospory. The production (after rain) of slime makes the diaspores adhere to the temporarily moist soil. MURBECK (1919) devoted the first part of his study to this phenomenon in the most divergent families; it is best expressed in Cruciferae, Compositae and Labiatae. The drier the climate, the more myxospermy there is.

ZOHARY (1937) distinguished 8 types of secretion but expressed doubt on its ecological significance for fixation, since in Palestine during the dispersal period the soil is sufficiently moist for quick penetration. STOPP (1958) found that, in a desert species of Oxalis, the nude embryo is expelled by explosion and is soon (after wetting by dew) enveloped in mucilage from the radicle, which afterwards dries and glues the embryo to the soil. In the slime the radicle develops very fast.

Another method of fixation (especially on loose soil) is the hygroscopic boring action (trypanocarpy) by alternation of drying and wetting in *Erodium, Stipa*, etc. ZOHARY (1937) described it for 48 species and confirmed the result, doubted by some authors, though he was again most specifically interested in its atelochorous aspect. The effectiveness stands in inverted relation to the effect of the awns for distant dispersal. In the geographic distribution good correlation exists with aridity, also in Australian and American species of *Erodium*. Many other atelochorous devices, such as geocarpy, provide fixation. Fixation may also determine the right position at germination.

C. Vivipary

This phenomenon, a growing-out of the embryo on the motherplant, bridges or oversteps fixation and germination. It may skip both, as it does dormancy. Vivipary is best known from mangrove plants such as *Rhizophora* and *Bruguiera* and is often classed as just barochory. Its function is then presented as a means to implant the embryo directly into the silt; fixation without dispersal. An objection is that at high tide this mechanism is void. Direct observation of the implantation has not been reported, as far as I know. One tends to doubt an opinion or observation ascribed to BEEBE, that the embryos are dropped at low tide only. One hardly finds seedlings growing underneath the mother tree, which can moreover not be expected in a rather dense edaphic climax.

Desert researchers, fascinated by atelochory, may consider the phenomenon as a means to avoid dispersal (near the sea by currents), as STOPP does for the viviparous *Oxalis* just mentioned, where fast germination is an important side effect in a dangerous, almost waterless environment.

On the other hand, vivipary has a clear relation to a water-habitat in the cases of floating embryos cited under hydrochory. Perhaps in those developed, nude embryos the essence is just superfluity of the testa, whereas atelochory is there redundant since the embryos float away. In the Araceae *Cryptocoryne ciliaris* (occurring in tidal mud) and *Aglaodorum griffithii* (found in fresh water) there is a real link with vivipary in the floating, further-developed embryos. We see real vivipary in some other mangrove plants, e. g. in *Aegiceras* and *Avicennia*, where the seeds germinate in the fruit, which then floats away.

In Australia, marine *Amphibolis antarctica* seedlings break free only when 7—10 cm long.

On the dispersal of *Rhizophora* much controversy exists after RIDLEY, but we may accept that floating is the rule and that under special circumstances the plantlets can strand, root, and erect themselves (EGLER, 1948).

In agreement with this opinion are the observed young *Rhizophora* vegetations, where all plants seem to have been established simultaneously at a certain distance from old trees. In Java the circular water movement at dead tide with a boring effect on vertical embryos, first described by EGLER, has also been observed. The vertical position is also obtained after dilution with fresh water.

It has been argued (JOSHI, 1933) that its vivipary has, nevertheless, as in desert plants, a relation with an endangered water balance. It might prevent germination of a vulnerable embryo on the surface of the silt where an extremely high salt concentration is found. In many other halophytes the young seedling is indeed less tolerant than the adult plant. MAYER and POLJAKOFF (1963) demonstrated this for *Atriplex halinus,* which halophyte is thus (like other ones) bound to dilution by rain for its germination. Indeed, the embryo of *Rhizophora* has a comparatively low osmotic value (about 20 atm, due to sugars) when compared to the mother plant (about 30 atm, due mainly to chloride). The embryo has to receive water by active secretion from the pericarp; indeed vivipary. According to BLUME (Rumphia 3) *Nipa fruticans,* from brackish tidal mud, has a beginning of vivipary. The fruits are not separated until germination is far advanced. This should be verified.

Although in *Cocos* we find development on the tree only in exceptional cases, the beginning vivipary of *Cocos* (p. 65) and of the Amaryllidaceae discussed below, also with a water reserve in the seeds, can be considered as promoting fast germination in a habitat poor in water. In the latter seeds, dormancy is skipped. So we return to the aspect of lack of usable water on the shore and in the steppe.

Some shore species of *Hymenocallis* have seeds with a thick, watery, vascularized integument. They burst through the pericarp at an early stage and the reclining shaft of the inflorescence deposits them on the ground. Some shore species of *Crinum* have comparable, testaless seeds, where the watery endosperm forms the reserve in a convergent way. The same vivipary happens in some South-African *Nerine* species from steppes. The radicle is often already visibile when the seeds with their watery, photosynthesizing integument are liberated. From the extensive literature I mention only some later papers, such as those by DUTT (in MAHESWARI, 1962) and WHITEHEAD and BROWN (1940).

Seeds of Loranthaceae, testaless and germinating on nude branches, also have a water reserve against the danger of the substrate. They can develop organs without help of outside water, even when fastened indoors on wood. The succulent vegetative bulbils of *Agave* and *Bryophyllum* also have more connection with fast germination in deserts than with atelochory. Probably they root faster than the seeds with distant dispersal. The atelochory is at most a side function. The vivipary of *Sechium edule* (REICHE, 1921), a cucurbitaceous plant from Central America, concerns a normal fruit, well known as a vegetable all over the tropical world. The juicy and slime-containing cucumbers are obviously without inhibiting substances. They let the single seed sprout when it is still enclosed and are planted as such. The sprout in the isolated fruit can reach a great length. This deserves physiological investigation.

There is no fundamental demarcation from so-called incidental vivipary of cereals, where normal seeds sprout precociously on the plant as a result of excessive humidity. In some species of *Inga,* this occurs so regularly that the bond with water or aquatic animals comes again to the foreground.

The conclusion on vivipary is, just as for geocarpy, that it is a phenomenon serving establishment in a wide range of environments with divergent origins. It may be based on just abolition of protection, desiccation, and the rest period. This is superfluous in water and unwanted during the favourable period in arid regions. The confusion is promoted by some handbooks which do not analyze the functional side and may include, like the one by ULBRICH, the false vivipary, which was excluded here on p. 10. Some even designate this as the true vivipary. MATTFELD (1920) illustrated the confusion and sought to escape by designating fructificative vivipary as "biotechnosis". This term is superfluous and is just a Greek translation of the Latin word "vivipary" (technosis = to bear).

D. Germination

1. General Importance

From dispersal we now shift to a field of its own with a rich literature (MAYER and POLJAKOFF, 1963). Some reconnaissance into this neighbouring field seems necessary, also because diaspores reflect so much of its characteristics, as became obvious in foregoing parts. The phase of germination is often the most critical one in the life of plants, and especially so in some communities where the diaspores, as a preparation for the seedlings, must be adapted to meet the requirements. WENT (1949) described how the floristic composition of desert areas in California is determined largely by rapidity of germination in the short periods of rain. The temperature optima for germination in such regions differ strongly in winter and summer annuals. When saying that the germination response determines the distribution range, such investigators over-estimate their field somewhat, just as old investigators of dispersal and pollination did for theirs.

KOLLER (1964) published a fine review article (77 items) on the survival value of germination-regulating mechanisms.

In aquatic plants, germination deep under water would be unlikely to lead to seedling survival, as MAYER and POLJAKOFF (1963) point out. Light requirement prevents this, favouring shallow places. However, in most instances of stimulation by light or even special light, the ecological function is not clear. This does not apply to light as a general condition in competitive germination.

STEBBINS (1950) pointed to the necessity of large diaspores in loose desert soil to make rapid formation of deep roots possible. Yet another demonstration of the manifold background of diaspore size and of germination influence on it!

In closed communities, the competition factor plays a role in germination, requiring resistance to many factors, and patience. SALISBURY (1942) showed for Britain a relationship between the seed weight of a species and the kind of habitat or stage in succession where it occurs. Those in woodlands are the heaviest, with the dispersal decreased in importance. For rain-forests this has been made evident before (for non-epiphytes). Selection there acts somewhat late in older seedlings with so-called advance growth. The case of *Mora*, with its gigantic seeds, was cited on p. 76. Thousands of $1^1/_2$-m high seedlings have to wait for their opportunity to obtain the full light they now need. *Quercus* and *Castanea* are also at home here but found a way to escape (p. 27).

In both kinds of woodland there are exceptions with smaller seeds (see the left column of Table 1) that do not require shadow for germination. SALISBURY called them "opportunists", VAN STEENIS (1956) called those in the rainforest "nomads". They are reservists meeting catastrophes by forming a secondary growth. The "nomads" may persist on the fringes in the climax, rarely surviving as high seed trees (*Pinus merkusii* in Sumatra). Here, too, germination limits can be narrower than those for further growth, so that near their upper limit (determined by germination) some trees grow optimally.

HARPER (in BAKER and STEBBINS, 1965) reported that plants *(Plantago)* introduced into meadows suffered from germination and establishment hazards that were innocuous for adults. The seedlings had to rely on favourable microsites. From this vast field of germination biology, we select a few topics for our purpose.

2. Span of Life and Dormancy

Dormancy has as a first function to prevent immediate germination, when the circumstances are still temporally favourable, and secondly to overcome an unfavourable period.

Longevity of diaspores must, as we have seen, be in consonance with the way of dispersal. It must also have a connection with the climate and its alternation of seasons. For exact data, I refer to CROCKER (1938) and

BARTON (1961). In the rain forest (see Table 1), the period of possible germination in open air is often (also in *Hevea*) over in a few days, always excepting the "nomads". The range in longevity of seeds of "escaped" species of *Quercus* and *Castanea* deserves to be recorded in a table. The seeds of European species are already known to be relatively short-lived, like beech and walnut. In America, red oaks are considered as having dormant acorns, in contrast to white oaks. The nomadic nature of wild *Musa* species is confirmed by the long-lasting dormancy of their seeds (SIMMONDS, 1959).

Especially in desert regions, the life span of isolated seeds and of complete diaspores of one species may differ greatly, a fact which should not be neglected, as demonstrated in the chapter on heterocarpy.

In sea-dispersed diaspores, where we saw salt as a menace to the embryo, the life span has been the subject of much study by GUPPY. The case of the lotos *(Nelumbo)* in fresh water is not exceptional. Estimates of the age of "seeds" buried in Japan and still vital vary, but point to some centuries. The hoaxes with "pyramid grain" have caused confusion among the public.

Archaeologists and geologists reported living seeds in layers up to 10.000 years old. For *Lupinus arcticus* see PORSILD e. a. (1967), for *Spergularia* and *Chenopodium* spp. see ØDUM (1965).

In cultivated cereals, agriculturists, anxious to grow as many generations in as short a time as possible and in every climate, have for millennia tried to overcome dormancy. One result was that wild cereals became a problem by remaining dormant in the field. Weeds have to be versatile in this respect, too.

The anatomical side of innate after-ripening is evident in (? primitive) seeds, where the embryo grows out after detachment. In Ranales this phenomenon persists even in Ranunculaceae, such as *Anemone* and *Ranunculus*. It also occurs elsewhere, as in *Ilex opaca* and *Fraxinus excelsior*.

Sometimes the seed germinates and produces roots, but the epicotyl remains dormant. This has been seen in species of *Asarum, Paeonia, Viburnum, Trillium*, and *Lilium*. In some Burseraceae and Leguminosae, dormancy starts after the unfolding of the primary leaves (pseudocotyls). Other innate mechanisms offer intermittent possibility of germination. Impermeability of the seed coat can mask this or override it.

3. Influence of Dispersing Agents and Other Stimuli

Inhibiting substances may be present in fleshy and dry diaspores. In deserts, rain often has to wash out the inhibitors which prevent germination after superficial wetting. The passage through animals can remove inhibition and influence the seed in other ways, as is known to cultivators. We found this already for reptiles, birds and ruminants; passage through the latter is especially needed to counterbalance the presence of an extremely hard coat on the seed. In America this is well-known for *Prosopis*. One curious case in an aquatic plant, that of *Potamogeton*, proves that this plant is not purely hydrochorous. Germination proved feasible only when all the factors imitating passage through birds were realized (LOHAMMER, 1954). I found a large difference in germination time between seeds of *Bixa* with and without pulp.

The influence of the accompanying dung is a point apart. In the case of *Cucumis humifructus* and the aardvark (p. 46), the dung is thought to be important. Mechanical abrasion of hard seeds during transport over sand and in the sea has been mentioned. The influence of some kind of light has already been discussed as potentially of ecological importance. Seeds of Loranthaceae require light so much that they die in darkness. In sociology it is important not to neglect the possibility that proven correlations with light may be based on germination requirements, not on requirements of the adult plant. We have to pass by further triggering of germination by all kinds of stimuli since this has little relation to dispersal. It should be mentioned that seeds can also inhibit each other (EVENARI, 1949 and later), and that leaf litter of one species can prevent the germination of other species both mechanically and chemically (a. o. the case of inhibiting *Brassica nigra* in California). It should also be mentioned that seeds may contain anti-biotics against microbes and repellants against insects.

Some words on the influence of fire, which is often important to promote germination of hard seeds and gives some tropical species of *Acacia* and *Albizzia* an advantage in burnt-off regions, thus determining the local floristic composition. This influence can even act in an earlier phase, namely on presentation. In Australia the woody, indehiscent (macrobiotic) fruits of some Myrtaceae *(Callistemon* and some species of *Eucalyptus)*, many Proteaceae *(Hakea)* and the cones of some Coniferae *(Callitris,* some species of *Pinus)* seem devoid of dispersal. After a bush-fire the fruits open, directly by heat or indirectly by the stopping of the water-supply to killed branches. The seeds remain arrested for a short time and then fall in a mass on the open, fertilized soil.

In the chaparral of California, the seeds of typical plants (*Rhus, Erio-dictyon, Ceanothus* spp.) are favoured by fire as a natural factor of importance (SWEENEY, 1956). "Fireweed" *(Epilobium angustifolium)* appears after forest fires, but only as a anemochorous pioneer, its germination being moreover, favoured by the light and ash abundantly available in the open places.

VIII. The Evolution of Dispersal Organs

A. Aims

The organs of dispersal in flowering plants will be discussed here from a special functional angle, namely the shift of functions in spores, seeds, and fruits. This approach will once more demonstrate the clash between different functions through the ages. It is essential to start with the pteridophytes, although these are not included in the main part. With all due respect to morphology, which has to work with given preceding structures, I hope to give a more functional background to changes in morphology and to the progression noticeable in diaspores.

Table 2 will be used as the basis of the following considerations.

B. Isosporous Pteridophytes

Four functions in the generative sphere will be considered here.

The spores carry the functions of (i) dispersal and (ii) dormancy (more or less pronounced).

The other mobile phase, that of the gametes, is responsible for the functions of (iii) sexual motility, providing genetical recombination, and (iv) sexual differentiation, coupled with sexual segregation.

In the lower part of the diagram (Table 2), which will be examined later on, they will again be found, differently arranged, together with more or less new functions of attraction: viz. (v) attraction for microspore-dispersal and deposition and (vi) attraction for dispersal of megasporangia (or seeds).

C. Heterosporous Pteridophytes

1. Forms with Free Megaspores

In the diagram the two functions come together (partly) in the horizontal tier marked "interphase". Here, the sexual differentiation of the gametes has shifted via the prothallia to the spores. It can be seen that the line of sexual shift crosses the line of dispersal shift, indicating that the haplont served both functions. The differentiation between male and female haplonts may also mean differentiation in dispersal, the one by wind, the other by water.

This schematic representation is a way to bridge mentally the gap between older isosporous Pteridophytes and the Pteridosperms c. s., apparent

Table 2. Crosswise shift of localisation of generative functions and their conflicts in plants

	Adult diplont	Sporangium	Spores	Haplont	Gametes	Resting young diplont	Fruit
Isoporous fern			Detached — Dispersal — Dormancy	Beginning sexual differentiation	sexual differentiation — sexual mobility	×	×
Necessary interphase I		Sexual differentiation	Heterospory	Sexual differentiation — Megahaplont dispersal in spore			
Seed fern		Sexual differentiation — Old megasporangium retained	Megaspore fixed, loss of dispersal	Megahaplont fixation on mother plant. Dispersal? by sarcotesta c.s.		?	?
Pre-angiosperm	Sexual differentiation		Distant sexual mobility by microspore			Seed dispersal by sarcotesta Dormancy	×
Interphase II						Seed dispersal disturbed	
Angiovulate	Sexual differentiation — New attraction					Sarcotesta arilloid	Fruit dispersal

Dormancy

after the crosswise shift of functions. How the meeting of functions in the interphase may have been realized in the haplonts is a matter for conjecture.

The evolutionary background of heterospory is usually seen from the sexual angle. Phaenotypical heterospory provides less mobile female spores, few in number but filled with food, and small, numerous male spores, mobile in wind or water. The properties of the macrospore are important for safer and faster germination of prothallus and zygote, whereas the microspores rely for their dispersal on safety in numbers.

This may be the primary background, rather than some differentiation or difference in dispersal, only the microspores by wind. In some mosses and in a normal leptosporangiate fern, *Platyzoma*, heterospory has been found independent of a special mode of dispersal, apparently only as an expression of genetical segregation in sexually heterozygous diplonts, leading to genetically determined unisexuality of haplonts.

A first handicap arises in the decreased chance of encounter between unisexual gametophytes. The other handicap, one frequently overlooked but of interest in the present context, is that the enlargement of the female spores means more and more the sacrifice of dispersal to distant sites. The first clash between functions! Warburg long ago pointed out that this situation in *Selaginella* calls for counter-measures. He connected it with the relict nature of diverse species that are confined to small areas. The improved catapulting of the heavy macrospores (some inches) in some species may provide some compensation.

It might be profitable to study the actual dispersal of a simple heterosporous plant of this type. In *Selaginella* there has been a suspicion that in the forest habitat of tropical species, which is rather windless, dispersal by the wind has been replaced by the scattering of megaspores or embryos by raindrops and rainwash (ombrohydrochory), as elsewhere.

It is remarkable that (as ZIMMERMANN, 1959, remarked) other recent heterosporous Pteridophyta *(Isoetes, Hydropterides)* also have links with water, which can transport large macrospores, macroprothallia, or still larger organs and bring microspores or microprothallia to them. MEEUSE (1961) already pointed out this circumstance, which also involves dispersal.

Species of *Isoetes* sometimes even have secondary complications on the reproductive organs, which arouses the suspicion that in ancient times there were possibly connections with animals to promote distant dispersal.

In the case of water ferns, there has been some discussion regarding their position in the basal stock of ferns. Their bonds with water concern both dispersal (including the gametophytic phase and the zygotes) and the easy meeting of more or less floating gametophytes for fertilization. This condition may be considered either as a survival of an early side-line in water, or as a later regression to this medium. Water-dispersal of female haplonts may occur inside sporangia or more elaborate organs. The puzzling switch to a more or less leptosporangiate condition and to a megaprothallium and an embryo situated outside the spore-wall should, in this view, be considered as induced secondarily by water-life.

The microspores may originally have reached the aquatic, floating macroprothallia by means of the wind, as in recent, newly aquatic plants. Water-dispersal of micro-spores seems here a specialized side-line due to regression, as it stands outside the mainstream of general progression, where microspores are kept in the air much longer.

The conclusion is (ecologically speaking) that this water-transport most probably evolved early in heterosporous Pteridophytes, before the general dominance of higher sporangia on land-plants with enclosed megaprothallia, pollinated by wind-borne microspores and already independent of soil-water for fertilization. A reversal in an end-line of real Pteridosperms (see MEEUSE, 1961) in order to escape from a lack of dispersal possibilities or other factors of extinction is also possible — as a comparison with higher plants returned to water shows.

To this we may add that their success in survival as ancient forms may have been assisted by secondary methods of dispersal: some of their anchoring and floating contrivances (hooks and slime masses) may also have served for animal transport. The more recent birds can later have extended the areas via those means (cf. RIDLEY). There are even papers pointing to the coupling of area-extension with migration routes of birds and of sporocarps inside birds.

2. Pteridosperms

When the macro(mega)spore and the prothallus remain enclosed in the macrosporangium, which in its turn remains attached to the mother plant, sexual differentiation has shifted far to the left in our scheme. There is no longer a real necessity for the female spore to be large, and the special spore wall becomes superfluous, although it persists in even higher groups. In most Gymnosperms it is, as a consequence, no longer separated from the surrounding tissue, though MARTENS found a layer of separating callose in Cycadales. Though seed-formation is clearly an ecological, polyphyletic convergence, some a-functionalistic botanists consider the non-separation of walls as primary, as the cause of seed-formation (cf. MARTENS, 1951). Palaeobotanists may decide (for seed-bearing Pteridophytes) whether the causal sequence is thus or the reverse.

Much attention has been paid to the sexual importance of this change to the seed habit. It frees the gametophyte from soil and water. I found less interest in the literature in organs secreting the water which is still necessary for fertilization.

Still less attention has been paid to the shift of the dispersal function to the right in the scheme — not even by THOMSON (1927), in an otherwise profound discussion of the seed-habit. This attention will now be paid.

The microspores provide no colonization of new sites. The macrospores lose their dispersal function entirely after their fixation in an attached sporangium.

In the scheme of Table 2, the four functions can be seen to be disrupted in a curious way, which results in such a major change that, in my opinion, it required an intermediate phase. Once again dispersal had to find a way out after being suppressed by sexual functions, which come first in ontogeny and perhaps in importance, especially in ferns. It might be better to say "the processes shifted their limits", as not only the newer haplontic and diplontic parts are dispersed, but also the old diplontic sporangia once they have served their sexual purpose. The macrosporangium had to provide transport to new sites. Simply rolling away (barochory) is a poor means of transport.

The choice is between dispersal (a) before, (b) after pollination, and (c) after fertilization, although all methods may have been followed together or separately in different groups.

The lack of visible embryos in fossil pteridospermous seeds is no sure indication of dispersal before fertilization, i. e. dispersal in the gametic phase. Zygotes are tender-walled and small and (as has been ascertained for Gymnosperms) a well-developed prothallium in a dropped, apparently mature, seed is perhaps no guarantee of fertilization. When growth in a rain forest is considered, the failure of dispersal and dormancy may have been unimportant, as said before, but elsewhere it must have hindered survival, together with other factors. This seems particularly so after the changes in climate in Carboniferous times when a shift in location became necessary (postulated in VAN DER PIJL, 1955). The sporangium and the later cupula have probably invented mechanisms to escape from this drawback.

Pteridosperms had become real land-plants and, though the sporangia may have been spread by rainwash and flushed into rivers, a general return to real hydrochory seems improbable. Neither the sporangium nor the cupula seems to be a floating apparatus.

The megasporangia seem, from the very beginning, too large for simple wind dispersal.

It is tempting to look toward animal dispersal for the large cupulae, macrosporangia, "seeds" or "ovules". It is impossible to form a meaningful opinion concerning the possible role of early insects.

The situation is, however, different in regard to endozoochory, in casu, by means of the early transitions to reptiles on the ground and to fish (for sporangia dropped or flushed into water). The swallowing may first have been an accidental one connected with the swallowing of foliage.

There is an early origin of a parenchymatous, probably fleshy, cover of the sporangia in Pteridosperms and even in those fossil Lycopodiales which show a tendency to the seed habit. The originally sexual functions of sporangial appendages (spore-collection or water-secretion) may have changed into dispersal functions. The morphology will be ignored here. A consideration of dispersal lends more meaning to swollen integuments and the like than the vague ideas of mere protection expressed by pure morphologists, who forget to say against what. The existence of a fleshy layer is not consistent with dispersal before pollination since digestion of the outer layers must have prevented pollination afterwards.

As said before, there is an early differentiation in the cover (perhaps convergently) into at least a juicy outer layer (sarcotesta) and a hard, protective, inner layer (sclerotesta). The protection may be against desiccation, crushing, and digestion.

D. Gymnosperms (or pre-Angiosperms)

We shall not enter into the discussion about where the limits are to be drawn between sporangium, ovule and seed, but mention the (simplistic) scheme of EMBERGER. According to this, Cryptogams are dispersed as spores, Prephanerogams as prothallia in ovules, and true Phanerogams as diplontic embryos in real seeds. For a critical discussion of this question, see MARTENS (1951).

In recent Conifers, one sometimes (still?) finds a sarcotesta *(Cephalotaxus)* or an aril, possibly differentiated from it as organogeny indicates *(Taxus)*, and even spurious fruits with diplontic auxiliary organs, — all for animal dispersal and even fragrant in *Cephalotaxus*. In *Pinus*, large, dry seeds fall into the ecological niche discussed on p. 26, which was later occupied by acorns and nuts. Many species of *Pinus* have small, anemochorous seeds, but their wings are accessory organs, not produced by the seed itself.

Ginkgo has greenish, drupe-like ovule-seeds with a faint smell, that fall to the ground. They have a juicy sarcotesta and a hard sclerotesta, which seems a continuation of the pteridospermous condition. Although their natural dispersers (reptiles?) may be extinct, it would be interesting to study their dispersal in the possibly remaining natural area. The dropping seems connected with dispersal, not with incidental pollination on the ground, as is often said.

We saw that recent Cycads are also mostly endozoochorous. In olden times, dispersal undoubtedly was brought about by the reptiles of the period (saurochory). Most *Gnetum* and *Ephedra* species also have zoochorous seeds.

Wind and beetles for the flowers, reptiles or fish for the seeds, such was the scene at the time! For this assumption there is factual confirmation.

WEIGELT (1930) described fossil reptiles from the Zechstein *(Protorosaurus)* with a mass of large, intact gymnosperm seeds in their stomachs. This does not point to destructive feeding, nor to accidental intake together with vegetative parts, but to a systematic gathering with resulting dispersal. The seeds were all of the same size, obviously collected when mature.

GUNDERSEN and HASTINGS (1944) wrote a popular paper on the interdependence of fossil plants and reptiles. After work of HEINTZE (1927) and ZAZHURILO (1940), Russian botanists also paid special attention to this point.

When the bond between animals and dispersal is compared with the one between animals and pollination, it can be seen that the first and oldest one remained one phase ahead during progression.

Table 3

	pterido-sperms	gymnosperms	angiosperms		
			early	middle	late
dispersal	reptiles ? wind	reptiles → birds and ? mammals	reptiles birds mammals	vertebrates wind exozoochory	vertebrates wind exozoochory autochory ants
pollination	wind	wind → beetles	beetles	hymenoptera beetles wind	hymenoptera wind vertebrates

E. Angiosperms

1. The Seed

We already discussed possible traces of the primitive situation in which Angiosperms were dispersed by vegetarian reptiles. In some groups *(Inga, Durio, Rosaceae, Ranales)*, there are still traces of a later bifurcation in dispersal.

The continuity of the character of seeds from Gymnosperms to Angiosperms is not entirely self-evident. In the latter group, the ovules are much more delicate, which may, however, be due to the enclosing and the disappearance of the large prothallium. The latter became triggered by pollination, not purely a specific one, even in its development of archegonia. When untriggered and not pollinated, and also after unspecific pollination, the prothallium becomes a waste, producing embryoless seeds (see p. 111).

Arguing for non-identity remains the fact that Angiosperms changed to an apparently different, secondary endosperm, triggered by (more specific and later) double fertilization as a new aspect (perhaps not entirely new). Some authors, therefore, considered it imperative to postulate an intermediate phase with no endosperm at all and the seeds consequently small (cf. HEINTZE, 1927). For this opinion there is no confirmation and the acceptance of HEINTZE's view, that families with small, scobiform seeds are primitive, leads to a strange consequence, e. g. to the idea that Orchidaceae and most saphrophytes are ancestral. TAKHTAJAN (1957) accepted the large seed as basic, but I cannot follow him when he considers decrease in size as advantageous in progression because it saves building material. We found many more reasons and also reversals; small and large seeds have many backgrounds!

The general primitivity of large, juicy seeds (megaspermy) has already been pointed out by CORNER (1949, 1953). It is one of the valuable aspects of his "Durian Theory", to be discussed later.

2. The Seed Escaped from Angiospermy

The further development of the sarcotesta-seed can be followed in Angiovulates (so-called Angiosperms), which enveloped their ovules in what will here be called carpels. We consider the sarcotesta as basically continuous. Broadly speaking, this envelopment is of a sexual nature, since it provides protection against side effects of pollinating beetles, protection against unwanted pollen by a kind of sieve (the stigma), germination and collection of pollen at special places, and so on. It has been sufficiently discussed before (among others by VAN DER PIJL, 1960—1). I shall not, therefore, pursue this sexual aspect now, noting only that its structural mechanisms were interpolated between ovule and seed-maturation.

The term "Angiosperms" seems incorrect, as it is not the seeds but only the ovules that are concerned in the sexual change in pollination. Seeds were only handicapped by envelopment and, as will be seen, originally even withdrew immediately from it in many cases. Their inherited dispersal scheme, biotic or abiotic, was again disturbed by the "sexual" process, so that the existence of an unbalanced intermediate phase should once more be postulated, this time between Gymnosperms and "Angiosperms". Secondary mechanisms became necessary for dehiscence of the envelope and exposure of edible and other seeds, later for transfer of attraction, and so on.

The handicap in dispersal in the first Angiovulates (see *Degeneria* on p. 110) may again explain, in part, their extinction. Later on, however, when real angiospermy had conquered the initial difficulties, the pluriformity of structures and methods for dissemination must have contributed to strong differentiation and to the success of the group in a new world with new dispersers.

Sexual difficulties may also have handicapped the first Angiovulates. The flowers had to find a niche in a biotic environment devoid of regular flower visitors. They could contact (and partly deceive) some beetles, but the bond was strongly synecological and vulnerable, bound to the environment as a whole, with irregular pollination, — until real flower visitors or reliable, stable connections of another kind had developed (see *Ficus* p. 121).

Maintaining the classical view on at least part of the ancestors of Angiosperms, we must now consider possible means of escape from the menace to dispersal caused by the closing up of carpels.

One means may have been early one-seededness by reduction concurrent with angiospermy, so that in the as-yet indehiscent fruit the carpel was incorporated into the seed. This is possibly the situation in primitive Calycanthaceae and Monimiaceae. There the hypanthium, however, provided a hip, which initially was useful in pollination (it is also present in male flowers), but was later utilized for attracting dispersing animals. Originally, the latter swallowed the whole. In Monimiaceae, this is still clear; the hypanthium there even dehisces like a fruit, though other structures may help in spreading the seed-like fruitlets. In *Calycanthus*, parts of the indehiscent, juicy hip may nowadays be taken (? with fruitlets) by birds (according to Dr. J. W. HARDIN, Raleigh) but the achenes are then not yet ripe. He considers the dried-out, untouched hip, still containing the fruitlets, as the mature "pseudocarp", which can be removed by squirrels.

These groups can be considered as being without juicy-fruited or many-seeded angiospermous ancestors; the sarcotesta and its derivatives were immediately suppressed. If the acarpellate concept for these groups were to be accepted, the clear relationship with other Polycarpiceae would become strained.

CORNER (1964: 212) considered one-seededness as a more or less orthogenetic, autonomous continuation of single-sporedness in the megasporangium and further reductions into singleness. Following this line of thought, one might also see it in Composites as an autonomous feed-back-regulation after an increase of flower number in the capitulum. However, with reference to the monovuly as discussed before, it seems necessary to point out that this change must have had a more realistic background, and that it is connected with too many ecological sources of pressure to be treated so simply.

Here again, monospermy seems a consequence of the constant clash between the functions of pollination and dispersal.

Most Polycarpicae (despite recent attacks still to be considered as primitive) maintained some form of sarcotesta (see p. 111).

I see no primary escape in Cyperaceae, where both anemophily of the flowers and hydrochory of the fruits seem to have contributed to secondary one-seededness. One-seededness of this latter kind by itself provides no support for an acarpellate origin. In general, it should not be thrown in with its early counterpart, as is likely to happen in statistical (numerical) treatments, more buttony than botany. Its three styles plead against acarpelly.

Another condition of escape from angiospermy still occurs in simple Angiosperms: the now superfluous covers of "carpels" are dropped or made to burst by the ovules as soon as these start to develop into seeds. On the other hand, the presence of this condition in certain families may prove their primitive nature. Here, too, the concept "fruit" does not yet seem to be applicable to the old ovary.

When considered from a physiological point of view, this condition might also be termed primitive; the transmission of building materials and auxins to the postfloral carpel-parts adjacent to the remaining placentas had not yet been perfected when their role in producing macrosporangia was fulfilled — as is the rule in organs producing microsporangia.

Such secondarily gymnospermous forms produce large, naked, coloured, berry-like, ornithochorous sarcotesta-seeds. Perhaps the definition "angio-vulate, not yet angiospermous" is better. Such seeds are found in Liliaceae (*Mondoideae*), Berberidaceae (*Caulophyllum*), Violaceae (*Decorsella* or *Gymnorinorea;* not ornithochorous are those on the open carpels of *Anchietea*). In Dioncophyllaceae (close to the Flacourtiaceae), the nude seeds are not ornithochorous, and neither are those in the nude-seeded Amaryllid-aceae discussed under vivipary on p. 96.

In some Celastraceae, the superfluous pericarp is simply thrown off later in the life of the fruit.

3. The Sarcotesta Maintained in Real Fruits

The polycarpiceous relic *Degeneria* has, though the closure of the carpel is incomplete, no dehiscence mechanism in its fruit and the juicy, reddish seeds (with sarcotesta) usually are liberated only when the fruit decays on the ground (cf. *Durio* and *Inga*).

In certain Sterculiaceae it is found, by way of a transition to what may be called a real fruit with angiospermy and dehiscence, that the carpels which have already fused before anthesis split apart and also open up shortly after pollination. Is the whole (an etaerio) a fruit or not? Ecologically, the open carpels form an escape from angiospermy. They expose the naked, ornithochorous sarcotesta seeds. This seems to be the basic condition in the family, from which the permanently syncarpous, indehiscent and fleshy pod of *Theobroma* is derived; the attraction, in the latter case, resides in a special pulp underneath the pericarp and around the seeds (see RIDLEY). CHEESMAN (1927) and others proved that the pulp is a sarcotesta formed from the outer integument.

A parallel temporary fusion of styles (and sometimes of carpel parts) for centralized pollination, with separation and splitting up after it, is well-known in some Rutaceae and Simarubaceae.

Many simple Polycarpicae in the tropics have follicles which re-open late without benefit of special structures; often passively by pressure from within, or by disintegration *(Talauma)*. In *Magnolia*, secondary, active dehiscence occurs along the "midrib". The organ, now really a classical fruit, still exposes the old coloured sarcotesta (also in *Michelia*). ZIMMERMANN (1959) is against the supposed primitivity of *Magnolia* and similar genera and denies that the seeds are simple because, among other things, they have such special, long funicles. In point of fact, there is no funicle at all. The thread from which they hang consists of uncoiled vessel-spirals from the raphe as has been known for a long time.

The same condition of secondarily exposed sarcotestas is found in other Polycarpicae, as in some species of Winteraceae, and Dilleniaceae, Bixaceae, Violaceae, Annonaceae *(Xylopia),* some Nymphaeaceae *(Euryale),* and so on. Also in higher groups to be described later.

Elsewhere (VAN DER PIJL, 1955), I mentioned the phylogenetical significance of Magnolia-like seeds, not knowing that ZAZHURILO (1940) had already stressed the link between *Magnolia* and Gymnosperms, and with saurochory, citing HEINTZE.

In the derived, temperate Polycarpicae (Ranunculaceae), more conventional forms of fruits and seeds have developed. Perhaps the elaiosome of *Helleborus* and the corky body on *Caltha* are remnants of a sarcotesta. The recently separated Paeoniaceae family still has beautiful ornithochory on the old basis. Often the opening follicles are still alive and thus show anthocyanins which lend colour to the attractive red valves, as these do to the seeds with their contrasting blue sarcotesta. Sometimes (see Fig. 3) there are special red, sterile seeds indicated as "show-seeds" (MILDBRAED, 1954). As dispersal by birds has been observed for species of *Magnolia* and *Paeonia*, it is not clear why PARKIN (1953) considers the colouring as probably nonfunctional. In fact, the attractive colouring (in some species) is almost the only functional, adaptive aspect of the primitive fruit, which in most cases opens up passively. I present a photograph of a Caucasian species (Fig. 3).

In the sterile seeds, consisting of a sarcotesta only, there is again a strong affinity to Gymnosperms. In *Ginkgo, Cycas, Podocarpus* and *Encephalartos*, similar sterile seeds containing endosperm only occur when foreign pollen reaches the ovule (VAN DER PIJL, 1955 and MARTENS, 1951). Swelling of integuments is there, obviously, independent of fertilization of the egg cell — a phenomenon worthy of study by fruit physiologists. The many fleshy but sterile seeds of *Degeneria* may be explained provisionally in a comparable way, by independence of the testa.

In some Euphorbiaceae, Meliaceae, Flacourtiaceae, Sapindaceae, and Palmae the thick sarcotesta is the edible part of popular table fruits (VAN DER PIJL, 1955, 1957 b).

Among Monocotyledones, one finds large sarcotesta seeds (eaten by man), covered by a thin, dry, finally bursting pericarp in some palms like *Zalacca* (Salacca) (see p. 22) in the Lepidocaryoideae.

The *Zalacca* condition seems unfavourable to the thesis of MEEUSE (1966) which considers palm fruits as "synspermia", fusion products of monovulate, cupulate and acarpellate seed-fruits. If, however, a juicy, arilloid sarcotesta is the homologue of a cupule, what can the pericarp be other than a carpel? The septal nectaries also conform to those of the Liliiflores.

Some basic Liliiflores (especially Melanthioideae as *Littonia* and *Gloriosa*), have exposure of berry seeds. Others (e. g. *Polygonatum* and *Majanthemum*) have the sarcotesta combined with a juicy pericarp (KRAUS, 1949).

In the genus *Paris* real berries occur, but also dry, dehiscing fruits with sarcotesta-seeds. In Himalayan *P. polyphylla* the latter are red and sweet, eaten even by man. The difference with nude-seeded Mondoideae is just one of time. Among Iridaceae, South African *Lapeyrousia*, the well-known temperate *Iris foetidissima* and the tropical *Belamcanda* expose berry seeds, with in some *Antholyza* species ornithochory expressed by vivid colours of valves and seeds. In some species of *Iris*, seeds continue to grow juicy and green even when uncovered artificially at an early stage; this shows that angiospermy is not essential.

The Leguminosae, in their more primitive representatives, also have exposed sarcotesta seeds. They will be treated separately in chapter IX.

Of course, one could also explain all these cases of a sarcotesta as adaptive convergence, without assuming genetical links with Gymnosperms. However, in my opinion the common roots emerging from basic stock are clear. The cases treated in this chapter belong to: Magnoliaceae, Annonaceae, Winteraceae, Degeneriaceae, Dilleniaceae, Paeoniaceae, Berberidaceae, Flacourtiaceae, Euphorbiaceae, Meliaceae, Sapindaceae, Leguminosae, Sterculiaceae, Violaceae, Bixaceae, and Violaceae. Further examples are provided by Liliaceae, Iridaceae, and Palmae (Lepidocaryoideae). A reversal of a hard testa with specialized palisade tissue to a parenchymatous testa seems improbable. One might try this explanation for the isolated cases of *Oxalis* (derived from a mucilaginous epidermis?) and the tomato, where this is really the case.

4. Arilloids

Further development in primitive fruits will be followed from a functional-ecological angle.

In the rain forest, the seeds of *Magnolia* and the like soon lose their power of germination, a weakness which seems unimportant there for climax-forms. For other plants it obviously became important to separate the two functions of attraction and hardness; these should no longer be manifest in two layers as before, but in two parts side by side. Then the juicy part can, moreover, be more easily separated after the transport.

This splitting of functions is reflected in local differentiation of the integument, with the larger part hard and dry, the smaller part juicy and a remnant of the total sarcotesta. BAILLON called such an appendage a localized aril. I prefer to call the juicy part an arilloid. The true aril seems an end product, not a starting point.

This is precisely the field treated by CORNER (1949; 1953) in his "Durian Theory": Modern fruits can be traced back to the fleshy red follicle with many large, arillate, nondormant seeds. He used the term aril very loosely, more in an ecological sense, for everything juicy near the seed, using only incidentally (for placental appendages) a morphological criterion. When meeting morphological discrepancies he rather freely invoked a process indicated by him as "transference of function" (see p. 119) defying homology.

It has sometimes been necessary for me to refer in a critical way to CORNER. With all due respect for his prophetic vision of the arillate fruit as primary, I merely want to take away fringes that hinder insight into the very valuable nucleus. I shall also use a more ecological approach, and in order to provide balance I will try to give the concept more of a head in front (somewhat reptilian since we have to deal with the sarcotesta) and a tail behind (the pulpa).

Arillus-like outgrowths on the seed can be found in four locations. Thus, we may find (see Fig. 24):

a) a small swelling on the raphe, a strophiole;
b) a small swelling near the micropyle, a caruncle;
c) an encircling structure around the exostome of the micropyle, an arillode, sometimes called false aril or exostome-aril;
d) a true aril, near the top of the funicle and thus around and next to the see proper.

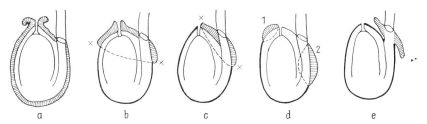

Fig. 24. Some arilloids in anatropous ovules as transitions from sarcotesta (a) to aril (e), via complete arillode (b) and partial arillode (c). In d 2 a strophiole, in d 1 a caruncle. Fleshy parts striped, outline on surface dotted, hilum as an ellipse

The latter condition is often hard to distinguish from a diffuse swelling of the free funicle part (in species of *Acacia*, Fumariaceae), a condition which may often be considered not as arilloid but as an incidental adaptive structure (see Fig. 4 and 5), especially when the whole is long and wound around the seed (as it is in Cactaceae), or when the swelling lies at a certain distance from the seed. This occurs in *Labichea* (Caesalpiniaceae).

According to this view, the aril is the most derived structure, with complete separation of the functions of hardness and juiciness. According to the classical compilation of PFEIFFER (1891), most arilloids belong to type c, and do not represent a real aril. I shall not treat the four classes separately here, as they have, naturally, too many links. Arilloids arise in groups with the sarcotesta as basis. LEENHOUTS (1958) accepted derivation from the sarcotesta in the Connaraeae, so near to the Leguminosae. I argued for such a derivation in Sapindaceae (VAN DER PIJL, 1957 a), as shown in Fig. 24.

In the tropics, arilloids are frequent in many families. CORNER (1953) has given us a list of so-called arils in 67 families, naturally incomplete but at the same time somewhat over-inclusive. The list of the dicotyledons contains, as CORNER remarked, the lower families. It is obvious to me that this rests on the older sacrotesta-basis as Fig. 24 suggests. Included are many Polycarpicae such as Annonaceae, Myristicaceae, Berberidaceae, Dilleniaceae, Nymphaeaceae, Aristolochiaceae, Flacourtiaceae, but also some examples from other parts of the system, Sterculiaceae, Papaveraceae, Capparidaceae, Amaranthaceae, Sapindaceae, Celastraceae, Polygalaceae, Bombaceae, Violaceae, Connaraceae, Lecythidaceae, Leguminosae, Rutaceae (see p. 116), and Meliaceae. The Saxifragaceae may be added *(Ribes)* (cf. KRAUS, 1949 and POHL, 1922), and also the Crossosomataceae.

"Arils" are even mentioned in the list for some sympetalous families such as Primulaceae, Hydrophyllaceae (see, however, under myrmecochory on page 49), and tentatively for some Rubiaceae and Apocynaceae, where, however, the soft mass is of a later convergent, placental or endocarpal origin (see below under "pulpa", p. 117). I fear that the assumed presence of an "aril" in the genus *Siparuna* (Monimiaceae) is due to a confusion of the fruitlet with a seed. KUHLMANN and KÜHN (1947) described an outgrowth from the receptacle around the fruitlets, acting as an aril.

The absence of Amentiferae is curious. The *"Salix"* in CORNER's list should be deleted since TAKEDA (1936) proved the placental origin of the hair tuft.

The seed-fringe in Asclepiadaceae is sometimes considered as an arillode, which seems exceptional in such a "terminal" family. Now seed-hairs occur in all kinds of higher anemochorous seeds. In the Asclepiadaceae they arise from the micropylar rim but also from the chalazal end of the seed, so that homology with an arillode is improbable.

Arilloids are found in many Monocotyledones, from Liliaceae to Zingiberaceae. CORNER (1953) has already commented on their absence in Helobiae, so primitive in other aspects and so much like Polycarpicae. Perhaps there is a remnant in some that are liberated, such as seeds of *Aponogeton* (soft, dehiscing testa) or *Hydrocharis* (the slime-hairs around seeds).

CORNER's colleague in Cambridge, SPORNE (1954), used the character "seed arillate" as a primitive one in his comparative statistical treatment of the evolutionary level of dicotyledonous families. He assigned the lowest advancement index to the Magnoliaceae (not in CORNER's list). The typical arilloids are found in families below the 50 % advancement index.

To return to ecology: generally speaking, arilloid structures are connected with ornithochory on a somewhat higher basis than the sarcotesta, with better dormancy in dry regions.

In some large fruits (which cannot be swallowed as a whole) the arilloid is eaten by man, who has taken over from monkeys and bats.

In temperate regions, botanists (including antiteleological ones such as GOEBEL) have often misjudged arilloids in the past, ascribing to them only the role of internal splitting of the pericarp by their swelling! In some Marantaceae (F. MÜLLER, 1883) these change into springy horns, propelling the seed; in *Phrynium*, this has led to myrmecochory. The aril may serve other secondary functions; in *Nymphaea*, e. g. it makes for hydrochory of loose seeds. In some Connaraceae and Meliaceae it acts as a funicle. Though over-generalization is dangerous, CORNER (1954) suggested it was probable that some anemochorous seed-wings are derived from arilloids in some capsular Sterculiaceae, Meliaceae, Bombacaceae, and Celastraceae. They may even be derived straightaway from the sarcotesta, as in some Leguminosae.

Many arillodes on anatropous ovules arise from the combination of an exostome-arillode with an aril from the hilar region. Then an 8-shaped double circle is the primordial phase. Is there coalescence of separate primordia of organs?

Because of this concurrence, there has been some doubt whether the difference between arillode and aril is significant. The aril is basal, the arillode terminal; the aril can overgrow the micropyle, whereas the arillode spares it in its centre. The aril is narrowly attached at the hilum next to the micropyle, the arillode is broadly attached on the seed itself and leaves (after detachment) a broad scar, the false hilum or pseudo-hilum of *Euonymus* and *Durio*.

A teratological observation seems to favour the idea of separate organs. For *Hitchenia caulina* (Zingiberaceae), PANCHAKSHARAPPA (1962) described how the combined aril-arillode of normal, anatropous ovules changed into separate rings in abnormal, atropous ovules; one ring being found around the micropyle and one around the funicle top (in MAHESHWARI, 1962).

How dangerous it is not to distinguish between aril and arillode is proved by the study of CAMP and HUBBARD (1963), who tried to homologize the vascularized "aril" of *Myristica* with the cupule of a Pteridosperm. It is, however, essentially not basal and not a true aril since it originates mainly around the micropyle. The vascularization seems, as in sarcotestas, of physiological significance.

In the literature (MAHESWARI, 1963), "obturators" from the outer integument are mentioned for *Coleonema* (Rutaceae) and *Rhus mysurensis* (Anacardiaceae). As these organs develop after fertilization, the term "obturator" seems better replaced by "arilloid".

Real obturators, guiding pollen tubes, arise early from diverse parts, often from the funicle. This occurs in higher families. In Combretaceae and comparable families confusion with an arilloid is possible. In *Ricinus* too the integumental caruncle arises before fertilization. The outgrowth of the inner integument of *Leukosyke* and *Myriocarpa* discussed as an important relic by MEEUSE (1966) may also be an obturator.

I shall let morphological discussion of this kind rest and will devote some more space to the Durian Theory. On p. 69, we already discussed CORNER's views (not those on tree-structure and leaves) but the feature of spininess, which apparently impressed him so much that he took as a type the durian *(Durio)* instead of his primeval "arillate red lantern fruits". CORNER's ideas were also reviewed critically by PARKIN (1953). I see that CORNER does start with *Sterculia* in his recent book (1964). The green durian (see p. 16 and 46) has no true aril but a combined aril-arillode, as is obvious from the gigantic pseudo-hilum on the seed. Its dehiscence is not of the primitive *Sterculia* type.

I repeat that CORNER's vision of fruits is, justifiably, tropically centered and basically correct. In my opinion, however, he did not begin at the beginning, neglecting the connection with Gymnosperms, which he believes to be non-existent.

In later papers (CORNER, 1953), he dismisses the argument (cf. VAN DER PIJL, 1955, 1956) that the sarcotesta is fundamental and considers it as derived, viz. as a coalescence of aril and seed (even for *Gloriosa* and *Magnolia*) or simply as a case of "transference of function of the aril".

The sarcotesta was, long before, considered to be a concrescent aril. As for the two families studied by me, the Leguminosae and Sapindaceae (VAN DER PIJL, 1956, 1957 a), anatomy and ontogeny do not sustain this notion.

One of CORNER's arguments was that the assumption that the sarcotesta is fundamental would make too primitive the Euphorbiaceae, which he consequently left out of his list of arillate families. SPORNE (1954) placed it low on his list. We met the family in the basic group on page 23.

Another argument was that the possible presence of a primary sarcotesta in Leguminosae must be denied because if it were present the strongly differentiated palisade testa would have gone back to a parenchymatous condition. We have seen, however, that it is present (see p. 123).

In temperate regions the arilloids present are almost exclusively (except in *Ribes* and Celastraceae) represented by the small caruncle and strophiole as elaiosomes. The link with ants is, as already said on p. 47, a relatively new one, still in the process of being developed and acting convergently; in most cases, though, it has clearly evolved from the sarcotesta and arilloids. In such Polygalaceae and Papaveraceae the evolution seems a reduction from large ornithochorous red arilloids (as in *Polygala* and *Bocconia* in the tropics).

The presence of an elaiosome in some Caryophyllaceae (species of *Stellaria* and *Arenaria*) does not prove their arillate character (see list of CORNER).

5. Pulpa

In accordance with CORNER and PARKIN, a further eco-morphological progression can be seen in the displacement of seed-coat activity to a more outward layer. In transitional cases this is not to the whole or outer pericarp but to a special outgrowth from the endocarp, its inner layer. The outgrowth, the so-called pulpa, penetrates between the seeds, thus forming a reminiscence or repetition of arilloids, within the tough protective outer pericarp. Thus the protective and attractive layers are again kept apart, with the attraction remaining internal, according to the old scheme. Dehiscence could remain as it was. Support for this concept is to be found in the fact that in some families arilloids and pulpa occur in one fruit or in alternate species (Musaceae, Marantaceae, Flacourtiaceae, Guttiferae, Sapindaceae, and some Annonaceae, such as *Xylopia* and *Artabotrys*). Even some Winteraceae already possess a pulpa. In some Guttiferae *(Garcinia, Symphonia)* pulpa and sarcotesta together form the edible layer, and in *Ribes*, pericarp, pulpa, sarcotesta and aril. The genus *Pithecellobium* (Leguminosae) has them all, distributed over various species.

What the taxonomical literature, however, mentions as pulpa is a chaotic mass, awaiting ontogenetic investigation. Especially so in Flacourtiaceae, Meliaceae, Pittosporaceae, Marantaceae, which all tend to arilloids. As early as 1874, BENTHAM pointed out this confusion in his revision of the Mimosaceae. Herbarium taxonomy has done little to improve it.

Some cases of a pulpa were, as was seen, included in CORNER's list of arillates. One of those, an "aril" in a sympetalous family (Apocynaceae), discussed especially by CORNER (1954), has to be struck off the list. Species of *Tabernaemontana (Ervatamia)* have a red pulp around the seed, apparently even around the funicle, which seems strange. In some Indonesian species this pulp covers a group of seeds and is an outgrowth of the pericarp from the placental region. It covers or, in the case of dangling seeds, supplants the funicle. In the Gardeniae (Rubiaceae) the whole endocarp forms a gelatinous mass around the seeds. This is a pulpa, not an aril. Some *Gardenia* fruits are reported as eaten therefore by monkeys and pigs and (in dehiscing fruits) by birds. We already mentioned *Genipa*.

The soft sarcotesta-mass around cocoa-seeds (cf. p. 110) has also often been termed a pulpa. In the banana, the edible mass is a real pulpa penetrating between the seeds. The fruit is descriptively considered as just a berry. In reality, it is a hesperidium as in *Citrus*.

The endocarp and its pulpa are important features in Leguminosae and Clusiaceae, and probably also in Loganiaceae, but they are best known in Rutaceae and the related Simarubaceae. In *Citrus* and *Aegle* the endocarp forms the edible mass. Sometimes *(Fagara)* it forms a layer around the seeds, acting as an aril which attracts birds (KUHLMANN nd KÜHN, 1947). Does the "aril" of the *Zanthoxylum* species, mentioned by CORNER (1953, 1964), belong here or is it really an aril as a basic organ in Rutaceae? *Coleonema* (see p. 116) would point in this direction but in the literature the juicy mass attached to seeds of *Zanthoxylum* has been described as a part of the placenta.

It has long been known that the clusiaceous and rutaceous endocarp can be split off tangentially as a varied organ in itself, leading to exposure and even autochorous propulsion of the seed (see p. 70).

The pulpa in Leguminosae will be described separately.

In other, higher, families the endocarp-pulpa acquired (convergently?) the function of the old aril so completely that it separates from the rest, e. g. in *Momordica* (Cucurbitaceae), where it forms the orange bags around the ornithochorous seeds. In other gourds, an endocarp layer clings to the seed.

Pulpy placentas filling up the space in dry pericarps, though morphologically farther derived, play a comparable role (Melastomataceae). This also necessitates a new term. This case can also be expected (cf. p. 49) in Hydrophyllaceae with their exuberant placentas.

6. The Pericarp-Fruit

Shift of Functions. The last phase in the evolution of dissemination organs is that seeds have lost all independent power of attraction and that this function (when maintained at all) has become entrusted to the pericarp together with that of early protection. It will be shown below that this phase was sometimes reached directly in early Angiosperms, by-passing the stage where the seed has the power to attract.

The process should not be seen simply as an orthogenetic outward shift. The new outer layer, the carpel, was plastic and could develop the necessary, secondary mechanisms that were denied to the seed. Its differentiation also means a further separation of the functions of early protection, attraction and late protection (with dormancy), which are now no longer situated in the seed alone. The endocarp can take over the function of late protection.

"Transference of function" (cf. CORNER, 1958) is a nice term to describe these processes, as long as it is not misused as a causal explanation and one does not suggest autonomous functions making wild jumps across gaps. This warning remains valid when one describes the transference as "genetic transference", a shift of gene activity to a different tissue. Perhaps morphogenetical research will reveal that the new layer may evoke and displace the activity of old genes for sarcotesta-differentiation. We saw that the palisade-layer of seeds can also originate from non-homologous layers.

The pericarp-fruit is mostly regarded as the normal fruit according to "temperate" concepts (I accept the risk that the first part of this chapter will now be considered intemperate). In fact, the ovary-products in this first part might be called "pre-fructus", with seeds still dominating functionally.

In studies of plant evolution the fruit is mostly neglected. This seems partly due to neglect of the previously described tropical and basic conditions and partly to inherent causes, as will be seen (p. 121). TAKHTAJAN (1959) devotes a separate chapter to it, later extended in the Russian edition of the first part of his book. He includes, as the first, some primitive fruits.

Often the pericarp desiccates and then dehisces by means of special structures, which are the main signs of progression here, together with late asymmetry and further postfloral differentiations.

It is now really an organ on its own! When the pericarp remains fleshy and alive, this may be either ecologically functional or not, a difference neglected in most phylogenetical considerations and fruit-systems, which merely distinguish between fleshy and dry. When the growing, living "carpels" simply remain succulent without special differentation and food-accumulation, the result may be defined as primary fleshiness, a simple lack of prematuration changes (as postulated already in VAN DER PIJL, 1955). Such fleshiness is found in primitive capsules and follicles (cf. p. 111), e. g. in *Sterculia, Euonymus, Paeonia, Macaranga*, and also in *Archidendron, Inga, Theobroma, Musa,* and Myristicaceae. At this point I must come to CORNER's rescue against one part of the criticism of PARKIN (1953) and the parallel objection of TAKHTAJAN (1959). Their objection to the senselessness of succulence and the power to attract of supposedly early fruit valves remains beside the point and shows a false understanding of ecology. A valve that remains fleshy and coloured may act as a visual signal. Drying out and dehiscence at special sites are relative progressions from the first condition. A slight physiological alteration in the time of desiccation and lignification may cause such changes *vice versa*. Again a warning to fruit-taxonomists!

In many cases, however, the pericarp becomes attractive and palatable as a whole, providing zoochory on a new basis and taking over the attractive function of the seed entirely.

In some groups the transition to an edible pericarp may have happened quickly in ancient times. *Sassafras* (Lauraceae) already possessed drupelets in the Lower-Jura epoch. Some Magnoliaceae, even *Drimys,* and many Annonaceae have already progressed to berries.

Autonomous Cycles. One could go on beyond the phase of the pericarp fruit, to spurious fruits or collective fruits with aggregation and further envelopment. If one had a tendency to philosophy, one could follow French botanists such as MANGENOT (1952) and see the progressive envelopment as a more less autonomous orthogeny, a cyclic development through the ages, each cycle with a phase of evolution, "surévolution" or involution. This tendency is admitted to be assisted by such factors as economy (reduction of seed-size) and selection in the floral phase. I agree that cupulate sorus, *Ginkgo*-seed, cherry, apple, and fig seem repetitions of the simple sporangium, but this is not simply, as MANGENOT thinks, because subsequent architectural processes have to follow the same course of evolution.

Whereas MANGENOT hardly discusses function, I prefer to consider the cyclic, sinusoid line of dispersal organs functionally — as produced by opposite selection-pressures, alternating in importance at different times, as described. This alternation can in the main have been between sexuality and dispersal, but at a lower level by changes in circumstances for pollination or dispersal, producing alternation between telechory and atelechory, dehiscence and non-dehiscence, many small seeds and one large seed, also by changes in the ovary. All this change means that every time there is again breakdown of the old way and escape into a new direction, often back to the last but one. The repetition of old organization schemes seems to me a repetition of answers to comparable environmental factors after foregoing change of the structures, suiting some other influence. Such repetition is not contradictory to DOLLO's Law as it concerns different morphological elements. This will be demonstrated in details for Leguminosae in the next chapter.

MANGENOT teaches us that development of a new enveloping organ causes compression of the earlier organ and that the type of Monimiaceae (as described on p. 109) or *Ficus* represents the contracted flower of the future.

In my opinion, the retardation and reduction in size of orchid ovules were not only related to the compression by overdevelopment of the flower, as stated by MANGENOT, but mainly to mycotrophy and old anemochory in the ancestry (cf. *Apostasia,* where the seeds are already reduced, though the flower is still simple).

Parallelisms and repetitions in flowers have also been indicated as autonomous. There too, ecological insight was able to refute such concepts (VAN DER PIJL, 1958).

Further Evolutionary Influences and Processes. At this point, having arrived at the "normal" fruit of modern times, some remarks on further evolution may be useful.

I shall not take up a stance for all incidental references to fruit evolution in angiospermous groups.

The first difficulty is that the higher development of the flower as a more centralized pollination organ has also influenced the ovary and thus the subsequent structure of the fruit, as has already been substantiated on p. 15.

For other reasons I doubt the possibility of finding general evolutionary trends in the life of the pericarp fruit itself — even if one agrees with the much-doubted monophyly in the origin of angiospermous ovaries and fruits. There seems to exist specialization in all directions, with regression and progression and an endless convergence.

EGLER (1943) gave a system of his own and mentioned 14 points of evolutionary progress in the fruit, meaning the common pericarp-fruit only. Most of these, however, refer primarily to the flower. These can serve for mere description and typological classification, but not for marking general evolution in the fruit.

EGLER's points 7 and 8 (many ovules or seeds against few) are mentioned as reversible, and thus are less important to us. Indeed, one-seededness can, as argued before, be just a pre-angiospermous remnant or a typical fruit-character, but then it may be either primitive *(Calycanthus)* or advanced. It can be connected functionally with the mode of dispersal, also with simple lack of dehiscence. It may also be just a flower character, a consequence of anemophily in the flower.

Some other points, low versus high, from EGLER's list refer to higher functions of the fruit itself — a kaleidoscopic array. One might add (see STOPP, 1950): symmetry of fruit unchanged from the original flower symmetry *versus* symmetry changed on its own. Also, homo- *versus* hetero-carpy (amphicarpy) and combination of tachysporous and bradysporous parts.

The intricate, spurious fruit of the old genus *Ficus*, placed high in his classification, is certainly not an end-product in the evolution of fruits. It is just a swollen inflorescence, as such indeed specialized, but pollinated by primitive wasps since primaeval times. It offers a closed breeding substratum to them. The combination of pollination and oviposition by one insect gave the stability mentioned on p. 109. The persistence and increase of fleshiness of the inflorescence wall after fertilization of its female flowers and the changing into a "fruit" even before male anthesis, provided a very simple regulation permitting endozoochorous dispersal after the preceding monovuly or monospermy.

My evaluation of these points as "progression" in the pericarp-fruit may be clear from the foregoing. They should not be applied to fruits in general, but to restricted groups where the floral aspect is of equal order. One should be extremely prudent as long as the possibility of acarpellate seeds and ovaries and the polyphyletic, convergent origin of carpellate structures has not been withdrawn from circulation.

IX. Ecological Developments in Leguminous Fruits

This review has a mixed character. It shows, first, the late plasticity of the fruit during speciation, acting also via dispersal. It is also to some extent a typological classification of the fruits, to some extent a trial in the direction of organ phylogeny, but in both respects with emphasis on the ecological background. We shall not enter into the eternal general question whether form or function is primary, but have here to emphasize the bonds with the biotic and abiotic environment. The review (already in VAN DER PIJL, 1956) must also try to maintain contact with current taxonomy, perhaps assist it. The result will show that, although the Mimosoideae again prove basic, it is possible to align the developments in the three sub-families, where the limits are sometimes vague.

Some words on the leguminous seed: continuing the work of CAPITAINE, PITOT and BOELCKE (1940), CORNER (1951) used special criteria to link and separate the old sub-groups anew. In his anatomical derivation, he somewhat neglected the functional differences and also the influence of non-dehiscence of the fruit, which may induce regressive reduction of the seed coat, not to be confused with primitivity. In his fear of premature ecological conclusions, he ascribed to the pulpa only the role of maintaining the turgidity of the embryo. I just mention his general conclusion to the effect that the papiliona-ceous seed is a specialization of the mimosoid-caesalpinioid seed. The Leguminosae are well suited for an inquiry into the ecology behind seeds and fruits, isolated from other processes, because the flowers are always entomo-philous (except in *Hardwickia*) and because their ovary is simple and uniform. The Cruciferae studied by ZOHARY (1948) at first hand for his country are equally interesting for a dispersal spectrum of a family, but are more complicated in possessing a more derived ovary.

Following the general lines in Chapter VIII, we shall see that initially the seed still dominates functionally in dispersal. The fruit in this first phase is a follicle, a container for seeds which themselves possess auxiliary organs. Later on, fruits evolved, which are descriptively listed as: drupe, samara, moniliform pod, lomentum, craspedium (a lomentum with persisting sutures forming a replum), achenium, utricle, legumen. Some queer, unnamed forms are: dry fruits with separating dry endocarp, fruits with a fleshy endocarp-pulpa, and a drupaceous lomentum with the hard endocarp jointed (crypto-lomentum).

One-seededness can be found with many backgrounds. As I said before, I reject the background of an orthogenetic trend to singleness, and also refuse to invoke "advancing sterility".

These forms have developed convergently in many tribes, where ecological specializations reign in a parallel way. Such groups are taxonomically considered as units (also as genera) for other reasons, mostly because of floral structure. BENTHAM, therefore, concluded in 1875 that fruit forms would not be used to split genera here. Instances of genera with very polymorphous fruits are *Acacia, Pithecellobium, Cassia* and *Erythrina.* Some authors, nevertheless, split genera with fruits as a criterion. The fruit-genera, apparently, do not yet overlap with floral genera.

We cannot sketch the differentiation within each floral genus separately, and can only occasionally trace the evolutionary trend therein, even though some genera (e. g. *Trifolium)* would fully deserve such treatment. For foregoing incidental remarks on them see the index.

The methods of dispersal in African Leguminosae have already been described by BUCHWALD (1895). His paper contains wrong assumptions based on herbarium-botany only: they have already been criticized by RIDLEY.

Connaraceae, possibly somewhat ancestral to Leguminosae, possess seeds with a sarcotesta and derived products and are basically ornithochorous too (LEENHOUTS, 1958).

We start with some primitive Mimosoideae, first the large genus *Inga* in South America. The data accessible to me are scarce and scattered, but it seems that we are here still at the simple level of beginning general zoochory with divergence according to a dispersal by fish, reptiles, birds and mammals. The seeds are uniformly surrounded by a white sweet pulp (also popular with man) which is easily detached from the nude embryo. I never saw an exact ontological investigation but most authors consider it as a sarcotesta, a transformation of the integument, although sometimes it adheres to the endocarp.

The sarcotesta-seed is not exposed. The whole fruit drops at maturity and does not dehisce. According to HUBER (1910) and KUHLMANN (1947), fish like the pods and these are often found drifting. Perhaps *I. aestuariorium* is in this way bound to river banks. The fact that the nude embryo is released points to water as an agent (cf. *Eperua* on p. 21). KUHLMANN found intact embryos of *I. sellowiana* in monkey excrements so that these (the embryos) seem protected chemically. In some species, the fruit dehisces more or less, or can be opened, and though not reported to be coloured, the seed is popular with birds. For *I. feuillei,* see BORZI (1903). Here the outside of the embryo is cutinized.

The anatomy of the pericarp has to my knowledge not been reported anywhere, and the presence of endocarp-fibres as a dehiscence-mechanism should be investigated especially. Perhaps *I. ciliata* forms a transition to an arilloid.

The Australian form, *Archidendron,* also florally primitive by its apo-polycarpelly, shows some torsion of the valves although often the process just provides side-slits. The red fruit with sweet sarcotesta-seeds is typically ornithochorous, just like the fruits of the *Sterculia* and *Paeonia* species mentioned on p. 111 (see Fig. 3). According to FAHN and ZOHARY (1955), the anatomy of the valve-layers is also of the simplest type. In this case, it seems primitivity, not the regression due to secondary indehiscence which they did not distinguish in their (descriptive) paper.

The pantropical genus *Pithecellobium,* related to *Inga,* is here considered *sensu lato,* neglecting the splitting into fruit-genera. Its evolution seems to start with ornithochory of sarcotesta-seeds, permanently exposed and some-times dangling on dehiscing or partly dehiscing valves, which are often coloured. Instances are *P. ellipticum* and *P. microcarpon* (with a red fruit). The torsion of the valves, caused by fibre-layers in the endocarp, seems functional as a presentation of berry-seeds, as is the case in other ornitho-chorous fruits.

In many species (such as *P. dulce, P. diversifolium*), the dehiscent pod presents arilloid seeds or (in *P. clypeatum* and *P. lusorium*) mimetic, blue seeds. When describing the seeds as exarillate, it is necessary to distinguish pre-arillate from post-arillate conditions.

Almost all other types of fruit mentioned in the beginning of this chapter have (? consequently) evolved in the genus, which apparently never produced a common legume for use outside forests. Pods, dropped for ground-ruminants are frequent *(Samanea).* Arilloids in these pods were abolished.

In the genus *Acacia,* sarcotesta and arilloid have in most species been replaced for ornithochory by the curious swollen funicles mentioned on p. 114. In other species, mainly African, the pod became indehiscent. Arilloids are superfluous there. *Albizzia* has a different aspect, with more anemochory and hydrochory and without arilloids.

The Piptadenieae represent a compromise, being high trees with pod-follicles that dehisce in one or two sutures, liberating without explosion winged, anemochorous seeds. These are exceptional in the family (and pointless in herbs). The wing of African species may be derived from a sarcotesta, of which the American representative *P. excelsa* still shows a trace.

In the sub-family of the Caesalpinioideae, arilloids are very frequent *(Afzelia, Copaifera, Sindora, Swartzia,* p. p.); they mostly serve for ornithochory, in *Swartzia proucensis* for dispersal by bats (cf. p. 44). The African genus *Schotia* even has some species with a primitive parenchyma-tous testa, not induced secondarily by occlusion. Many species have arilloids, but a craspedium (replum) also occurs (PITOT, 1960). *Cassia* has abandoned the use of arilloids and specializes in pulpa fruits for mammals, but also has lomenta, legumes and even a winged, ballistic "Rinnenhülse" in *C. alata.*

The Papilionideae show a different seed development, aimed more in the direction of dormancy and help from the pericarp. They tend to varitaion in the pod itself, the range often being extended to form a legume. This is not the basal type, although it is fixed in the European mind as such. Its autochory is a sign of a pioneer-character, prevalent in herbs and shrubs. Its twisting endocarp is just a newly utilized remnant of the *Archidendron* condition. Sometimes vestigial arilloid structures are left; these are usually referred to as strophioles. They may be remnants of an arilloid or of a funicle top as in *Acacia*. In some forms *(Stizolobium)* it is still large.

We are now gradually leaving the genial, humid environment, as leguminous trees had to do in many regions after geological, climatological changes.

Some Leguminosae had to find a compromise between seed-attractivity and strong dormancy. A way out was the deceit discussed as mimesis on p. 37, which maintained ornithochory of the seed although the latter grew very hard and dormant.

As said there, the imitative type arose on a sarcotesta — or arilloid — basis, not entirely *de novo*. The occurrence of this type in all three subfamilies points to a model of old stock, to ecological parasitism on preexisting berry-seeds. Even the Papilionideae found this way, perhaps especially they, as exemplified by the best known case: that of *Abrus precatorius* as the single representative of its genus. The genus *Ormosia* has predominantly "coral seeds" (hormos = necklace). The derivation is simple when we consider *Arillaria*, indicated by CORNER as a priceless relic from Burma for his "Durian Theory", but taken over here as such to parade as our saint. It is in all other points an *Ormosia*, but has a juicy layer around the seed, called aril by CORNER, although probably a sarcotesta as in *Archidendron*. There too, taxonomists call it an aril. The relic is, alas, too rare to have it dissected for a decision. The yellow seeds of the Amazonian forms O. *excelsa* and O. *macrocalyx,* being liberated only after the dropped, indehiscent fruit has rotted away, deserve ecological investigation.

In *Erythrina,* mimesis developed in many species all over the world. I could not trace concurrence with taxonomic sections and variance in habitat. The genus has further developed all possible kinds of fruit for many modes of abiotic dispersal, neglecting the mammals. *E. lithosperma* has hemi-legumes, each half forming an anemochorous samara.

In some sections of the Papilionoid genus *Rhynchosia*, we find an alternation of mimesis with the presence of small, dark seeds with the white structure near the hilum which in floras is indicated as a strophiole. The specific names occurring in this group, "cantharospermum" and "scarabaeoides", refer to the likeness of the seeds to beetles. In old works, this likeness has been considered as mimetic too, but the condition is more likely to prove myrmecochorous — if indeed accompanied by early presentation to the ground. In some other Papilionideae, myrmecochory developed on this basis (see p. 49), on top of autochorous explosion. Investigation of possible deceit in regard to insectivorous birds, too, is necessary. In some basical Sophorae *(Baphia, Leucomphalos, Bowringia)* permanently attached coral seeds, red or bicoloured, are found with strophiolae. Are such strophiolae elaiosomes?

Here the principal role of seeds ends. The fruit-wall takes over completely. We have already encountered this phenomenon in pulpate zoochorous fruits in savannah regions, which are swallowed by ruminants, monkeys, etc. (see p. 118). A transition may be assumed when the pulpa clings separately to the seeds, which are picked individually by birds. OSMASTON (1965) and others observed this in *Parkia filicoidea* (Mimosoideae).

The pulpa is present in the three sub-families, in some species of *Cassia, Dialium* and *Gleditschia.* It probably is already in existence in some species of *Inga,* such as *I. jinicuil* and *I. densiflora.*

In *Swartzia* and *Pithecellobium,* the pulpa alternates with arilloids. Traces of endocarp prolification are still visible in *Vicia* and *Phaseolus.* The endocarp separates from the rest as an anemochorous wing in *Schizolobium* and as a hard layer underneath a fleshy pericarp in *Pithecellobium* species.

The pericarp as a whole can in diverse groups become semi-fleshy and the fruit indehiscent for use by ruminants, etc. *(Tamarindus, Ceratonia).* This happened to a large degree in African *Acacia* species. In diverse tribes of the Papilionideae and Ceasalpinioideae, it can even change into a real, juicy drupe, edible for man *(Gourliea, Detarium).*

Many such plum-like pods have in nature been seen to be dispersed by bats *(Dipteryx odorata, Andira inermis, Cynometra cauliflora, Inocarpus edulis).* For *Holocalyx glaziovii* and *Cordyla africana,* this type of dispersal is very probable, seeing that the pod can even produce the typical fermentation odor attractive to bats. The few caulicarpous leguminosae also possess this type of pod in almost all cases.

The one-seeded fruit has returned to the situation existing in *Cycas* seeds, as in a cycle of MANGENOT.

Development of an explosive pod was easy by utilization of the torsion in exposing valves. It developed most frequently in herbs as an autochorous way out, but occurs also in high forest trees, with large seeds lacking dispersal devices thrown many meters away. The genera *Castanospermum, Pentaclethra* and *Brachystegia* represent the three sub-families.

The lomentum, breaking into indehiscent joints, occurs in various groups. The effect is mostly hydrochory and (in adhesive joints) epizoochory (see *Mimosa* on p. 81).

Reduction of seed number and of the testa is a natural consequence of indehiscence and transport of the whole.

Non-dehiscence of dry pods, combined with one-seededness, can lead to wind-dispersal of circular samaras (*Derris* and *Dalbergia* spp.) or ordinary samaras *(Myroxylon)*. In trees or lianas, a slight change can make these relatives, in those genera that live on shores, become river- or sea-dispersed. Also in *Pongamia* and *Cynometra ramiflora*.

The Papilionideae are, from the floral viewpoint, the most derived forms requiring a very precise bee-pollination. The seeds and fruits are often also derived, mostly by simplification. The Papilionideae in the above-mentioned groups with drupes, samaras and water-dispersed pods (in *Dalbergia* and *Sophorae*) show indehiscence and monospermy as part of their respective dispersal-syndromes. It would be going too far to investigate which was the primary factor in the deviation from the dehiscing, polyspermous pod.

The more temperate tribes stick to autochory by exploding legumes, for use in pioneering herbs in cold or dry regions. For incidental adaptations in deviating circumstances, also for epizoochory, they provide further modifications and also accessory organs such as swollen or toothed calyxes (see p. 73).

Some fruits change into lomenta, some into ballistic organs (see p. 72), burrs or small, one-seeded achenes (see *Trifolium* below). Obviously, this is not an autonomous cycle. In very arid regions the fruits show the reductions in dispersal described before. The giant genus *Astragalus* (1600 species) was already mentioned under various headings. ZOHARY (1939) analyzed 100 oriental species, ballists, rollers, one-seeded calyxfruits and the typical hemilegumes where the septum provides two halves as independent diaspores.

The same author (1937) already mentioned briefly the evolutionary development of synaptospermous devices in the group of Papilionideae-Trigonellae in Palestine, a trend culminating in monospermous, indehiscent pods. Such forms can switch to anemochory or to epizoochory (see *Medicago, Trifolium, Astragalus, Adesmia* in the foregoing parts).

Table 4 represents a short recapitulation of the main groups. It omits the partly hypothetical oldest relations (with reptiles) and the most peripheral ones (with ants). The scheme suffers from the impossibility of using more than two dimensions. The first vertical column is certainly not to be considered as a linear sequence.

Many one-seeded pods are eaten together with the foliage by horses and cattle and the pods or seeds excreted in the dung, as is known for many species of *Medicago, Melilotus* and *Trifolium*. Other regulative ways of dispersal occur after one-seededness, especially after aggregation (for floral purpose) and after specialization in the calyx.

This situation might, in agreement with MANGENOT, be seen as the beginning of a new "autonomous cycle," of contraction followed by new

Table 4. *Review of leguminous pods*

Morphological classes	Ecological classes						
	Birds	Bats	Ground mammals	Autochory	Wind	Water	Exozoochory
Seed attractive, pericarp ± dehiscent ± fleshy a) Sarcotesta	*Archidendron* *Pithecellobium* *Inga*	? *Inga*	*Inga* p.p.				
b) Mimetic seed	*Abrus* *Adenanthera* *Pithecellobium* *Afzelia*						
c) Aril or arillode		*Swartzia*					
Seed dry, pericarp indehiscent, fleshy d) Mesocarp dry, endocarp pulpa	*Parkia* sp.		*Gleditschia* *Swartzia* *Cassia* p.p.				
e) Drupe	*Ceratonia*	*Ceratonia* *Cordyla* *Cynometra*	*Tamarindus* *Prosopis* *Acacia* spp.				
Seed dry, pericarp dry f) Pericarp dehiscent, not explosive				*Cassia alata* *Astragalus* spp.	*Erythrina* spp	*Erythrina indica* *Caesalpinia bonducella*	
g) Pericarp dehiscent, ± explosive				Legumen, many non-tropical spp.			
h) Pericarp indehiscent, large					*Dalbergia* p.p. *Oxytropis*	*Vigna marina* *Pongamia*	*Clitoria laurifolia*
i) Pericarp indehiscent, seed-like			*Medicago* *Melilotus* *Trifolium* p.p.		*Astragalus* p.p. *Adesmia* p.p.		*Medicago* p.p. *Astragalus* spp. *Desmodium* p.p.
j) idem, accessory envelopment					*Trifolium* p.p. *Astragalus* p.p.		

envelopment, of the one-seed achene by the persisting calyx, with the latter often taking over the dispersal functions, casually helped by a withered corolla. With their queerly shaped calyces some *Trifolium* species (e. g. *T. clypeatum*) approach in the pseudofruit the fruit of the Compositae. The

Fig. 25. Postfloral heads of Trifolium piluliferum (Israël) with some slit-up, pappus-like calyces, showing the single seeds out of the thin, papery pods. (Photo NATAN)

basal part of the calyx encloses the pod (often papery) and the part above the constricted throat sticks up and out like a pappus, often feathery in appearance (see Figs. 23, 25, 26). Pod and calyx-base might fuse in the future. In conjunction with the presence of involucral bracts in some species and the aggregation into heads, this new ecologism suggests initiation of "Papiliocompositae" as a family of future taxonomy.

We also see again monospermy accompanied by condensation, and indeed in some cases the whole infructescence of *Trifolium* functions as one dispersal unit (roller or geocarp). There even exists already some differentiation within the head, for example in *T. globosum* and *T. subterraneum,* where the central flowers are abortive and change into bristles (boring or hooking). After having speculated in Chapter IV on a preluding influence of dispersal upon the flower of Compositae (in the calyx-teeth) we can now, after the experience with *Trifolium,* strengthen this view. Probably the calyx, in that

Fig. 26. Inflorescence and postfloral head of Trifolium clypeatum (Iraël). Some (detached) fruit-calyces isolated to show likeness to pappose fruits of Compositae. (Photo NATAN)

case too, was initially loose, with a differentiated upper part for dispersal. Later on, the latter maintained this function, whereas the enveloping lower part fused with the fruit. In still later developments, it did so, as a prelude, with the ovary. According to this view, inferiority of the ovary may have started with the fruit in Compositae, although floral influences may have assisted (see p. 17). The site of nectar-secretion can decide whether or not such anticipating (preluding) inferiority of the ovary is adverse to the function of the flower. This clash between dispersal and pollination was avoided in the early Compositae and Rubiaceae and in the Vaccinium mentioned on p. 17, where the glandular part of the torus was raised. It is as yet unavoidable in *Trifolium* and also in Labiatae, though here too the calyx persists and assists in dispersal.

X. Man and his Plants

Many plants owe their distribution in some respect to man. They have all been indicated as anthropochores, in a wide sense. This is too wide a sense, as man is not the direct agent of dispersal for all of them, only producing the right substrate. The unfortunate use of "anthropochores" for "antropophytes" causes strange sentences like: "we found a high percentage of anemochores in anthropochores" (Sissingh).

Seen from the historical, floristic-regional standpoint, new arrivals are indicated as adventive plants or neophytes. The latter term is, however, often reserved for entirely naturalized species, (perhaps arrived naturally), that are at present independent of human activity.

The grass *Spartina townsendi* is a neophyte in a double sense, being a new, amphidiploid, species which conquered new territories in tidal mud in Western Europe by natural means.

The old, popular term of weed has a confused content, but weeds have, naturally, some connection with mankind.

NAEGELI and THELLUNG (1905), gave a classification of weeds in genetic groups, designating all plants bound to man and his actions as anthropophytes. The term "anthropophiles", used as a collective noun, should be avoided because of nomenclatural confusion with pollination-classes. Under the name of "apophytes", the above authors lifted out a group composed of those native plants that switch in mass to places influenced by human habitation; the remainder of the weeds they considered to be the true anthropochores. The s. c. ruderal plants consist of native and introduced plants bound to special habitats, often created by human activity. They may, therefore, be classified vaguely under anthropogene vegetation or as anthropophytes. Early man selected a number of cultivated plants from ruderals growing spontaneously near his dwellings, but these are as a group not necessarily anthropochores. The concept of weeds as small plants is not generally valid, as *Prunus serotina* already shows for Europe. The inhabitants of tropical secondary forests may be indicated as woody weeds.

In recent years sociological, floristic classification has been tried (TÜXEN, 1966).

The term anthropochores could also be applied to plants introduced intentionally, but not connected with human activity in their further dispersal and distribution because natural dispersers took over. Instances are bird-dispersed *Lantana camara* in Java and *Prunus serotina* in Europe, both discussed before, and also the introduced anemochores and other escapees from gardens.

We may also omit all cultivated plants (as long as they do not spread spontaneously), since their dispersal seems to lie outside our chosen field, but on the other hand plantgeographers have to consider them as anthropo-

chores outside their natural regions. Historical studies in this field we have
to leave aside, but these, on their side, have to reckon with dispersal ecology,
amongst others with the capacity of parts to survive travel in the company
of man and to travel spontaneously. Even a short discussion of the puzzles
around the origin and dispersal of *Nicotiana, Zea, Lagenaria, Cucurbita,
Ipomoea, Gossypium* etc. would be out of place here.

The changes effected during long cultivation, and the reconstruction of
the genetic make-up of the original diaspores also belong to the biological
side of such studies.

Earlier, we saw that the functions of dormancy and dispersal were often
discriminated against in agriculture. Certain natural properties of diaspores,
such as the disintegration of cereal spikes, the synaptospermy of *Beta,* the
dissemination of seeds in flax and poppies, the presence of seeds in oranges
and the penetrating odour of bat-fruits (in wild-type *Mangifera* species),
were simply a nuisance to man. The same holds for the natural dispersers,
that were mentally degraded to the rank of robbers (e. g. bats in the case
of dates). Cultivated *Zea* has become an "impossible" plant during its
domestication, and is now devoid of all natural dispersal ability. Knowledge
of natural pollinators and dispersers cannot be dispensed with in studies
concerning the geographical origin of cultivated plants. Examples are *Musa
Fehi* (VAN DER PIJL, 1956), and *Artocarpus incisa* (VAN DER PIJL, 1957)
in Hawaii.

Our main interest, however, lies in our involuntary companions, the
weeds, or more generally and neutrally described, the fast colonizers of new
territories.

The effect exerted by man lies firstly in the new open habitats he creates.
The opening of arable land in a forested region like Java found few natural
weed-candidates, since most plants were shadow-loving, with the exception
of some natural pioneers. The country was overrun by invaders, now 300.
An early list of these contains 65 Americans, 25 Europeans, 16 Asians,
5 Africans and 1 Australian, as well as many of uncertain origin. RIDLEY
gave a comparable list for Singapore. MULLIGAN (in BAKER and STEBBINS,
1965) reported on the mainly European, weedy invaders in Canada which
are dominant over much of the settled area. He stressed their wide range of
tolerance, their polyploidy (46 % of the 150 most common weeds) and the
ability of their seeds to germinate at any time when favourable circumstances
are present.

In sunny California, native opportuniy was left open, but there was a
large influx from the eastern Mediterranean region. STEBBINS (in BAKER and
STEBBINS, 1965) estimated that the hundreds of weeds in agricultural regions
there, established since 1750, comprise about 40 apophytes with colonizing
tendencies, partly composites. Levantines were long adapted as weeds.

In Europe, colonization by "anthropochores" is so old that an evaluation of individual cases is difficult and can often be based only on bonds with disturbed soil. GODWIN, in a history of the British flora, has shown that much of the weed flora was present in glacial times before the arrival of neolithic man, though early flowering summer annuals seem to be post-glacial.

New Zealand was a paradise for invaders, which have transformed the vegetation within a century. In 1949 the number of aliens, naturalized since 1799, was about one thousand.

The other side of the picture is presented by the plants, in their aggressiveness. In order to be successful, they must, of course, possess means of abundant seed production and fast dispersal, but this is not the whole truth. The list of the most successful weeds of our planet contains not only those "focusing" on dispersal mechanisms; their genetic make-up must also be suited to the special requirements. This more modern viewpoint was the topic of a recent symposium, already referred to (BAKER and STEBBINS, 1965). STEBBINS postulated here that there exists no relationship between the size of a native genus and its chance of producing a weed, so that special, preadaptive properties seem necessary. BAKER discussed some large genera of the composites possessing seeds with a pappus (*Tridax, Eupatorium, Ageratum*) finding each with but a single or a few species, especially annuals, that act as weeds.

We must here pass over the discussed general plasticity, the advantage of certain breeding systems (selfers preferred), of a certain ploidy-level, of the possibility of adaptation to day-length, of the length of the life-cycle, of reproductive capacity and of germination-potential.

The relation between a high ploidy-level and aggressivity has also been studied by PIGNATTI (in TÜXEN, 1966). The level proved to be equal in pioneers in natural and anthropogenous vegetations, and a high level is assumed to have been effective in reconquest after glaciation.

We might add as a factor in aggressivity: unselective pollination.

The apparent superfluity of or lack of interest in dispersal in sociological work, cited before, is illustrated by the contribution of E. POLI in TÜXEN (1966), a book on weeds. *Oxalis cernua* is described there as forming a dominant in an association in Sicily, without reference to its sterility and its curious dispersal (see p. 12).

This limitation notwithstanding, we cannot forego paying some more attention here to the transport factor, — which after all is also part of the plant's genetic constitution. ZOHARY, Jr. discussed, in the symposium, a group of "wheats", namely 24 *Aegilops* and *Triticum* species. The three dispersal mechanisms most successful in the original diploids under different climatic conditions were the only ones met in the polyploids, other genetic combinations being evidently nonsense-combinations.

Dispersal plasticity of weeds was already mentioned as an important factor under the topics of heterocarpy and polychory. The many remarks on the harmony between habitat and dispersal need not be repeated and listed here in relation to weeds. The connection with man and agriculture may also have brought about changes in them, sometimes converting a weed into a crop-plant.

In MÜLLER-SCHNEIDER (1955), we find data on *Sonchus* species, originally purely anemochorous but gradually shifting to anthropochory by adhesion, during long contact with agriculture.

Weeds growing among crop plants, (e. g. in fields of cereals and flax) had to conform to these in many respects, as one can easily learn from a comparison with the wild forms. The general habit, the period and periodicity of germination and maturation, the size of the seeds are curiously similar, in fact almost identical. VAVILOV applied here the term "mimicry", already misused so often for non-ecological likeness.

A third aspect of importance in the development of colonizing weeds must be their escape from natural competitors and antagonists.

Often a species with a small area, apparently immobile though possessing means of dispersal, shows explosion into a weed after artificial translocation (e. g. *Solidago multiradiata* in Montreal). Perhaps the old habitat was a refugium with immobilisation, with factors inhibiting ecesis beyond a minimum. In the new habitat the old dispersal-possibility obtains full expression. The old condition was no proof that dispersal-mechanisms are redundant in general.

Many adventive plants owe their new distribution to the trade in grains and wool. The fleece of sheep can carry burrs, farther transported with the wool. The history of the migration of *Xanthium* into South-America and Australia is ted up with the migration of sheep. *Medicago denticulata*, after its introduction into Australia became, as "burr-medic" obnoxious to the wool trade. The migration of weeds in crops is, likewise, not immediately anthropochorous and is not even epizoochorous. The main factor, overriding the transport of the products by man, is their being suited to the conditions for the crop, plus a certain likeness of their diaspores to those of the crop. All alien plants, indirectly connected with human activity for their distribution and/or dispersal, were indicated in Finland (by LINKOLA) as hemerochores (hemero = tamed or civilized).

The anthropochores *sensu stricto* cling to man and his gear as just a case of special epizoochory. This involves few new principles, and readers interested in an enumeration of cases and historical details, are, therefore, invited to consult RIDLEY or the works dealing with alien elements in each national flora. The book by THELLUNG (1930) also is a rich source of information on weeds.

The intricate analysis of anthropophytes or synanthropes can be summarized in the following scheme:

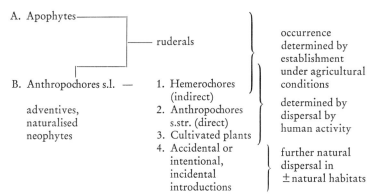

A. Apophytes

            ruderals

                                    occurrence
                                    determined by
                                    establishment
                                    under agricultural
B. Anthropochores s.l. —   1. Hemerochores   conditions
                               (indirect)
   adventives,   2. Anthropochores   determined by
   naturalised   s.str. (direct)   dispersal by
   neophytes   3. Cultivated plants human activity
                            4. Accidental or
                               intentional,   further natural
                               incidental   dispersal in
                               introductions   ± natural habitats

References

Accorsi, W. R., 1953: Biology and ecology of the Podostemonaceae of the Piracicaba Fall. Proc.7th Int.Bot.Congr.Stockholm, 681—682.

Aragao, A. de, 1947: Pescarias fluviais no Brazil. Sâo Paulo: Clements.

Atsatt, R. R., 1965: Angiosperm parasite and host: coördinated dispersal. Science 149, 1389—1390.

Baker, H. G. and G. L. Stebbins (editors), 1965: The genetics of colonizing species. New York-London: Acad.Press.

Bancroft, H., 1930: The arborescent habit in Angiosperms. New Phytol. 29, 153—275.

Barkman, Jos., 1958: Phytosociology and ecology of cryptogamic epiphytes. Assen (Netherl.): v. Gorcum.

Bartels, E., 1964: On Paradoxurus hermaphroditus. Beaufortia 10, 193—201.

Barton, L. V., 1961: Seed preservation and longevity. London-New York: Hill.

Baumann-Bodenheim, M. G., 1954: Prinzipien eines Fruchtsystems der Angiospermen. Ber.Schweiz.Bot. Ges. 64, 94—112.

Beal, W. J., 1898: Seed dispersal. USA.

Beccari, O., 1890: Malesia, 3. Firenze.

Becker, H., 1913: Über die Keimung verschiedenartiger Früchte und Samen bei derselben Species. Beih.Bot.Zbl. 29, 21-143.

Benl, G., 1937: Eigenartige Verbreitungseinrichtungen bei der Cyperaceengattung Gahnia. Flora 131, 369—386.

Berg, R. Y., 1954: Development and disperal of the seed of Pedicularis silvatica. Nytt.Mag.Bot. 2, 1—60.

—, 1958: Seed dispersal, morphology and phylogeny of Trillium. Skr.norske Vid. Akad.Oslo (Math.-nat. Kl.) 1958 (1).

—, 1959: Seed dispersal, morphology and taxonomic position of Scoliopus, Liliaceae. Skr.Norske Vid.-Akad.Oslo, M.-N.Kl. no.4.

—, 1966: Seed dispersal of Dendromecon: its ecologic, evolutionary and taxonomic significance. Amer.J.Bot. 53, 61—73.

Bews, J. W., 1917: The plant succession in the Thornveld. S.Afr.J.Sci.14, 150—160.

Bhandari, N. N., 1963: Embryology of Pseudowintera colorata. Phytomorph. 13,

Boelcke, O., 1940: Estudio morfologico de las semillas de Leguminosae. Darwiniana 7, 240—322.

Borzi, A., 1903: Biologia dei semi di alcuni specie d'Inga. Att. Accad.naz.Lincei 12, 131—140.

—, 1911: Ricerche sulla disseminazione della piante per mezzo di sauri. Memorie Soc.ital.Sci.nat. (3) 17.

Bresinsky, A., 1963: Bau, Entwicklungsgeschichte und Inhaltsstoffe der Elaiosomen. Biblioth.Botan.nr. 126, Stuttgart.

Brodie, H. J., 1955: Springboard dispersal operated by rain. Canad.J.Bot. 33, 156—157.

BUCHWALD, J., 1895: Die Verbreitungsmittel der Leguminosen des tropischen Afrika. Bot.Jahrb. **19**, 494—560.

BURKART, A., 1943: Las Leguminosas argentinas. Buenos Aires: Acme.

BURTT, R. B., 1929: A record of fruits and seeds dispersed by mammals and birds from the Singida district of Tanganyika territory. J.Ecol. **17**, 351—355.

BURTT, B. L., 1961: Compositae and the study of functional evolution. Trans.Proc. bot.Soc.Edinb. **39**, 216—232.

CAMP, W. H., and M. M. HUBBARD, 1963: Vascular supply of the ovule and aril in peony and of the aril in nutmeg. Amer.J.Bot. **50**, 174—178.

CAMPAGNA, G., 1905: Contribuzione alla storia litteraria della disseminazione. N.G.Bot.Ital. **12**, 657—671.

CARLQUIST, S., 1966 a: The biota of long-distance dispersal, II. Loss of dispersibility in Pacific Compositae. Evolution **20**, 30—48.

—, 1966 b: The biota of long-distance dispersal, III. The Hawaian Flora. Brittonia **18**, 310—335.

CHEESMAN, E. E., 1927: Fertilization and embryogeny in Theobroma cacao. Ann. Bot. **41**, 170—215.

CHETTLEBURGH, M. R., 1952: Observations on the collection and burial of acorns by jays in Hainault. Brit.Birds **45**, 359—364.

CLEMENTS, F. E., 1905: Research methods in ecology. Lincoln: Univ.Pub.Co.

CONSTANCE, L. (edit.), 1963: Amphitropical relationships in the herbaceous flora of the Pacific coast of North and South America: A symposium. Quart.Rev.Biol. **39**, 109—177.

CORNER, E. J. H., 1949: The Durian theory or the origin of the modern tree. Ann. Bot.II. **13**, 367—414.

—, 1951: The leguminous seed. Phytomorphology **1**, 117—150.

—, 1953: The Durian theory extended — I. Phytomorphology **3**, 465—476.

—, 1954: The Durian theory extended — II. Phytomorphology **4**, 152—165.

—, 1958: Transference of function. J.Linn.Soc.London Bot.**56**, 33—40.

—, 1964: The life of plants. London: Weidenfeld.

CROCKER, W., 1938: Life-span of seeds. Bot.Rev. **4**, 235—274.

CRUDEN, R. W., 1966: Birds as agents of dispersal for disjunct plant groups of the temperate Western hemisphere. Evolution **20**, 516—532.

DAMMER P., 1892: Polygonaceenstudien. I. Die Verbreitungsausrüstungen. Engl. Bot.Jahrb. **15**, 260—285.

DANSEREAU P., and K. LEMMS, 1957: The grading of dispersal types. Contr.Inst. bot.Montreal No. 71.

DAWSON, E. Y., 1962: The giants of Galapagos. Nat.Hist., N.Y. **71**, 52—57.

DIEREN, J. W. VAN, 1934: Organogene Dünenbildung. The Hague: Nijhoff.

DOCTERS VAN LEEUWEN, W. M., 1929: Kurze Mitteilung über Ameisen-Epiphyten aus Java. Ber.dtsch.Bot.Ges. **47**, 90—99.

—, 1936: Krakatau. Leiden: Brill.

—, 1954: On the biology of some Loranthaceae and the role birds play in their life-history. Beaufortia (Amsterd.) **4**, 105—208.

EGGELING, W. J., 1955: The relationship between crown form and sex in Chlorophora excelsa. Emp.For.Rev. **34**, 294.

EGLER, F. E., 1943: The fructus and the fruit. Chronica bot. **7**, 391—395.

—, 1948: The dispersal and establishment of red mangrove, Rhizophora, in Florida. Caribb.Forester **9**, 299—320.

ERNST, A., 1934: Das biologische Krakatau-Problem. Vjschr. Naturf.Ges.Zürich **59**.

EVENARI, M., 1949: Germination inhibitors. Bot.Rev. **15**, 153—194.

FAEGRI, K., and L. VAN DER PIJL, 1966: Principles of pollination ecology. Oxford: Pergamon.

FAHN, A., and M. ZOHARY, 1955: On the pericarpial structure of the legumen, its evolution and relation to dehiscence. Phytomorphology 5, 99—111.

FEEKES, W., 1936: De ontwikkeling van de natuurlijke vegetatie in de Wieringermeer-polder. Ned.Kruidk.Arch. 46, 1—295.

FIRBAS, F., 1935: Über die Wirksamkeit der natürlichen Verbreitungsmittel der Waldbäume. Natur und Heimat 6 (3), 1.

FLOWIK, K., 1938: Cytological studies of arctic grasses. Hereditas 26, 430—440.

FOSBERG, F. R., 1948: Derivation of the flora of the Hawaiian islands. In: ZIMMERMANN: Insects of Hawaii. 1, 107—119.

—, 1951: The American element in the Hawaiian Flora. Pacific Sci. 5, 204—206.

GALIL, J., 1965: Vegetative dispersal of Allium ampeloprasum. II. Isr.J.Bot. 14, 184—191.

—, 1967: On the dispersal of the bulbs of Oxalis cernua by mole rats (Spalax ehrenbergi). J.Ecol. 55, 787—792.

GESSNER, F., and L. HAMMER, 1962: Ökologisch-physiologische Untersuchungen an den Podostemonaceen des Caroni. Int.Rev.ges.Hydrobiol. 47, 497—541.

GINDEL, I., 1960: Biological function of fruit. Nature (Lond.) 187, 42—44.

GOBY, C., 1921: Classification génétique des fruits des plantes angiospermes. Ann. Inst.Ess.Semenc.Jard.bot.Republ.Russe 4, 1—30.

GRANT, V., 1958: The regulation of recombination in plants. Cold Spr.Harb.Symp. quant.Biol. 22, 337—363.

GREENHALL, A. M., 1956: The food of some Trinidad fruit bats. Suppl.J.Agric. Soc.Dept.Agric.(Trinidad).

—, 1965: Sapucaia nut dispersal by greater spear-nosed bats in Trinidad. Carrib. J.Sci. 5, 167—171.

GRESSIT, J. L. (editor), 1963: Symposium Pacific Basin Biogeography. Honolulu: Bishop.

GUNDERSEN, A., and G. T. HASTINGS, 1944: Interdependence in plant and animal evolution. Sci.Mthly.(N.Y.) 59, 63—72.

GUPPY, H. B., 1906: Observations of a naturalist in the Pacific. II. Plant-dispersal. London: Mc. Millan.

—, 1912: Studies in seeds and fruits. London: McMillan.

—, 1917: Plants, seeds and currents in the West Indies and Azores. London: Mc. Millan.

GUSULEAC, M., 1938: Zur Präzisierung der Nomenklatur der Früchte und der Prinzipien eines natürlichen Fruchtsystems. Bul.Fac.Sti.Cernauti 12, 337—355.

GUT, B. J., 1960: Beiträge zur Morphologie des Gynoeceums und der Blüten einiger Rutaceen. Bot.Jahrb. 85, 151—247.

HAWKES, J. G. (editor), 1966: Reproductive biology and taxonomy of vascular plants. Symposium B.S.B.I. Oxford: Pergamon.

HEGEDÜS, A., 1948: A termesek osztalyosa (The classification of fruits). Borbasia 8, 62—75.

HEIMANS, J., 1954: L'Acessibilité, terme nouveau en phytogéographie. Vegetatio 5,6, 142—146.

HEINTZE, A., 1927: Cormofytermas fylogeni. Lund: Selbsverlag.

—, 1932/35: Handbuch der Verbreitungsökologie der Pflanzen. Stockholm: Selbstverlag.

HILDEBRAND, F., 1873: Die Verbreitungsmittel der Pflanzen. Leipzig: Engelmann.

HUBER, J., 1910: Mattas e madeiros amazonicas. Bol.Mus.Goeldi 6, 91—225.

JANCHEN, E., 1949: Versuch einer zwanglosen Kennzeichnung und Einteilung der Früchte. Oesterr.bot.Z. **96**, 480—485.

JONES, E. W., 1955: Ecological studies on the rain-forest of Southern Nigeria. I. J.Ecol. **43**, 564—594.

—, 1956: idem, II. idem 44: 483.

JOSHI, A. C., 1933: A suggested explanation of the prevalence of vivipary on the sea shore. J.Ecol. **21**, 209—212.

KADEN, N. N., and M. E. KIRPICNIKOW, 1965: A possible contemporary system of fruit-terminology. Taxon. **14**, 218—223.

KEAY, R. W. J., 1957: Wind-dispersed species in a Nigerian forest. J.Ecol. **45**, 471—478.

KLIMSTRA, W. D., and F. NEWSOME, 1960: Some observations on the food coactions of the common Box Turtle (Terrapene c. caroline). Ecology **41**, 637—647.

KNAPP, R., 1954: Experimentelle Soziologie der höheren Pflanzen. Stuttgart: Ulmer.

KOLLER, D., 1964: The survival value of germination-regulating mechanisms in the field. Herbage Abstracts **34**, 1—7.

KOSTERMANS, A. J. G. H., 1958: The genus Durio. Reinwardtia **4**, 47—153.

KRAL, R., 1960: A revision of Asimina and Deeringothamnus. Brittonia **12**, 233—278.

KRAUS, G., 1949: Morphologisch-anatomische Untersuchung der entwicklungsbedingten Veränderungen an Achse, Blatt und Fruchtknoten bei einigen Beerenfrüchten. Oesterr.bot.Z. **96**, 325—360.

KREFTING, L. W., and E. ROE, 1949: The role of some birds and mammals in germination. Ecol.Monogr.**19**, 271—286.

KUHLMANN, M., and E. KÜHN, 1947: A flora do distrito de Ibiti. Publçoes Inst. Bot.Secr.Agric., Sâo Paulo (B).

LEENHOUTS, P. W., 1958: Connaraceae. In: Flora Malesiana. Leiden.

LEEUWEN, W. M. DOCTERS VAN: see DOCTERS VAN LEEUWEN.

LEVINA, R. E., 1957: (Russian title). Means of dispersal of fruits and seeds. Moscow.

—, 1961: (Russian title). On the classification and nomenclature of fruits. Bot.Zh. SSSR. **46**, 488—495.

—, 1967: (Russian title). The aspects of investigation of heterocarpy. Bot.Zh. SSSR. **52**, 3—12.

LOHAMMAR, G., 1954: Matsmältningens inverkan pa Potamogetonfrönas groning. Fauna och Flora **1/2**, 17—32.

MAC LEOD, F., 1891: Lijst van boeken, verhandelingen over verspreidingsmiddelen der planten. Dodonaea (Gent) **3**, 192—231.

MAHESWARI, P. (editor), 1962: Plant embryology, a symposium. Delhi: C.S.I.R.

—, 1963: Recent advances in the embryology of Angiosperms. Delhi.

MANGENOT, G., 1952: L'Evolution de l'ovule, du pistil et du fruit. Année biol. III **28**, 149—162.

MARTENS, P., 1951: Les préphanerogames et le problème de la graine. Cellule **54**, 105—131.

MATHENY, W. A., 1931: Seed dispersal. Ithaca: Slingerland.

MATTFELD, J., 1920: Über einen Fall endocarper Keimung bei Papaver somniferum. Verh.bot.Ver.Prov. Brandenburg **62**, 1—8.

MAYER, A. M., and A. POLJAKOFF-MAYBER, 1963: The germination of seeds. Oxford: Pergamon.

MC ATEE, W. L., 1947: Distribution of seeds by birds. Amer.Midl.Natural. **38**, 214—223.

MEEUSE, A. J. D., 1958: A possible case of interdependence between a mammal and a higher plant. Arch.neerl.Zoöl. 13, 314—318.

—, 1961: Marsileales and Salviniales — "Living fossils"? Acta bot.neerl. 10, 257—260.

—, 1966: Fundamentals of phytomorphology. New York: Ronald.

MILDBREAD, J., 1964: Die Schausamen von Paeonia corallina. Ber.dtsch.bot.Ges. 67, 73—74.

MÖBIUS, M., 1940: Die vegetative Vermehrung der Pflanzen. Jena: G. Fischer.

MOLINIER, R., and P. MÜLLER, 1938: La dissémination des espèces végétales. Rev. gén.Bot. 50, 53 e. s.

MUENSCHER, W. C., 1936: The germination of seeds of Potamogeton. Ann.Bot. 50, 805—821.

MÜLLER, P., 1955: Verbreitungsbiologie der Blütenpflanzen. Verh.Geobot.Inst.Zürich, 30. Bern.

MÜLLER-SCHNEIDER, P., 1959: Ist Chenopodium album eine prähistorische Nutzpflanze? Bericht 1958 Geobot.Inst.Rübel, Zürich.

—, 1967: Zur Verbreitungsbiologie des Moschuskrautes (Adoxa moschatellina). Vegetatio 15, 27—23.

MURBECK, Sv., 1919/20: Beiträge zur Biologie der Wüstenpflanzen, I, II. Lunds Univ.Arsskr. 15 (10), 17 (1).

NAEGELI, O., and A. THELLUNG, 1905: Die Flora des Kantons Zürich, I. Die Ruderal und Adventivflora. Vjschr.Naturforsch.Ges.Zürich 50, 232—305.

NORDHAGEN, R., 1932 a: Zur Morphologie und Verbreitungsbiologie der Gattung Roscoea. Bergens Mus.Arbok.1932. N.R.no. 4.

—, 1932 b: Verbreitungsbiologische Studien über einige europäische Amaryllidaceen. Bergens Mus.Arbok 1932 N.R.no. 5.

—, 1932 c: Über die Einrollung der Fruchtstiele bei der Gattung Cyclamen und ihre biologische Bedeutung. Beih.Bot.Zbl.Erg.Bd. 49, 359—395.

—, 1936 a: Verbreitungsbiologische Studien über einige Astragalus und Oxytropis Arten der Skandinavischen Flora. Ber.Schweiz.bot.Ges. 46, 307—337.

—, 1936 b: Über dorsiventrale und transversale Tangentballisten. Svensk.Bot.Tidskr. 30, 443—473.

ØDUM, G., 1965: Germination of ancient seeds. Dansk Bot.Ark. 24 (2).

OSMASTON, H. A., 1965: Pollen and seed dispersal in Clorophora and Parkia. Commonw.Forestry Rev. 44, 97—105.

OVERBECK, F., 1925: Über den Mechanismus der Samenabschleuderung von Cardamine impatiens. Ber.dtsch.Bot.Ges. 43, 469—475.

PARKIN, J., 1953: The Durian theory — a criticism. Phytomorphology 3, 80—88.

PPEIFFER, H., 1891: Die Arillargebilde der Pflanzensamen. Bot.Jb. 13, 492—540.

PHILIPPS, J. F. V., 1926: General biology of the flowers, fruits and young regeneration of the more important species of the Knyska forests. S.Afr.J.Sci. 33, 366—417.

PIJL, L. VAN DER, 1955 a: Sarcotesta, aril, pulpa and the evolution of the angiosperm fruit, I, II. Proc.Ned.Acad.Wet. (C) 58, 307—312.

—, 1955 b: Some remarks on myrmecophytes. Phytomorph. 5, 190—200.

—, 1956: Classification of the leguminous fruits according to their ecological and morphological properties. Proc.Ned.Acad.Wet. (C) 59, 301—313.

—, 1957 a: On the arilloids of Nephelium, Euphorbia, Litchi and the seeds of Sapindaceae in general. Acta bot.neerl. 6, 618—641.

—, 1957 b: The dispersal of plants by bats. Acta bot.neerl. 6, 291—315.

—, 1958: Flowers free from the environment? Blumea (Suppl.) 4, 32—38.

PIJL, L. VAN DER, 1960/61: Ecological aspects of flower evolution. Evolution 14, 403—416; 15, 44—59.

—, 1966: Ecological aspects of fruit evolution. Proc.Ned.Acad.Wet. (C) 69, 597—640.

—, and C. H. DODSON, 1967: Orchid flowers, their pollination and evolution. Miami: Univ. Press.

PITOT, A., 1960: Etude comparative des graines de quelques espèces du genre africain Schotia. Bull.Inst.Fr.d'Afr.Noire A, 22, 1200—1230.

POHL, F., 1922: Zur Kenntnis unserer Beerenfrüchte. Beih.Bot.Zbl. 39, 206—221.

PORSILD, A. E., C. R. HARINGTON, and G. A. MULLIGAN, 1967: Lupinus arcticus Wats. grown from seeds of pleistocene age. Science 158, 113—114.

PRAEGER, R. L., 1913: Buoyancy of the seeds of some Brittannic plants. Sc.Proc. roy.Dublin Soc. 14, 13—62.

QUISUMBING, E., 1925: Stony layers in seeds of Gymnosperms. Bot.Gaz. 79, 121.

READ, R. W., 1960: Palmfruits as bird food. Principes 4, 31—32.

REICHE, K., 1921: Zur Kenntnis von Sechium edule. Flora 114, 232.

RICHARDS, P. W., 1952: The tropical rain forest. Cambridge: Univ.Pr.

RICK, C. M., and R. I. BOWMAN, 1961: Galapagos tomatoes and tortoises. Evolution 15, 407—417.

RIDLEY, H. N., 1930: The dispersal of plants throughout the world. Ashford: Reeve.

RÜBEL, E., 1920: Die Entwicklung der Pflanzensociologie. Vjschr.Naturforsch.Ges. Zürich 65, 576.

SALISBURY, E. J., 1942: The reproductive capacity of plants. London: Bell.

SCHIMPER, A. F. W., 1891: Die Indo-malayische Strandflora. Jenna: Fischer.

SCHMIDT, TH., 1918: Die Verbreitung von Samen und Blütenstaub durch die Luftbewegung. Oesterr.bot.Z. 67, 313—328.

SCHUSTER, L., 1950: Über den Sammeltrieb des Eichelhähers (Garrulus). Vogelwelt 71, 9—17.

SERNANDER, R., 1906: Entwurf einer Monographie der europäischen Myrmekochoren. Uppsala: Sv.Vet.Ak.Handl.

—, 1927: Zur Morphologie und Biologie der Diasporen. N.Acta Reg.Soc.Sc.Uppsaliensis, Uppsala.

SIMMONDS, N. W., 1959: Experiments on the germination of banana seeds. Trop. Agric. 36, 259.

SPALDING, V. M., 1909: Distribution and movements of desert plants. Carneg.Inst. Wash. Publ.no. 113.

SPORNE, K. R., 1954: Statistics and the evolution of dicotyledones. Evolution 8, 55—64.

STEBBINS, G. L., 1950: Variation and evolution. New York: Columbia.

STEENIS, C. G. G. J. VAN, 1933/36: On the origin of the Malaysian mountain flora. II. Bull.Jard.Bot.Buitenz. 13, 289—417.

—, 1956: De biologische nomaden-theorie. Vakbl.Biol. 36, 165—173.

—, 1962: The land-bridge theory. Blumea 11, 235—372.

STEPHENS, S. G., 1958: Factors affecting seed dispersal in Gossypium and their possible evolutionary significance. N.Carol.Agr.Exp.Sta.Techn.Bull. 131.

STOPP, K., 1950: Karpologische Studien I—IV. Abh.math.-nat.Kl. Akad.Wiss.Mainz 1950 (7): 165—210, 495—542.

—, 1956: Botanische Analyse des Driftgutes vom Mittellauf des Kongoflusses mit kritischen Bemerkungen über die Bedeutung fluviatiler Hydatochorie. Beitr.Biol. Pflanzen 32, 427—449.

STOPP, K., 1958 a: Die Kongolesischen Arten der Labiaten-Gattung Aeolanthus mit zygomorph dehiszierenden Fruchtkelchen. Beitr.Biol.Pflanzen 34, 395—399.

—, 1958 b: Die verbreitungshemmenden Einrichtungen in der Südafrikanischen Flora. Botan.Studien 8, Jena.

—, 1962: Antitelechore Einrichtungen bei den Gattungen Sesamum, Rogeria und Psilocaulum. Beitr.Biol.Pflanzen 37, 63—76.

SVEDELIUS, N. E., 1904: On the life-history of Enalus acoroides. Ann.R.B.Gard. Peradenyia 2, 2.

SWANBERG, P., 1951: Food storage, territory and song in the Thickbilled Nut-cracker. Proc.10thInt.Ornithol.Congr.: 545—554.

SWEENEY, J. R., 1956: Reponses of vegetation to fire. Univ.Calif.Publ.Bot. 28, 143—250.

TAKEDA, H., 1936: On the coma or hairy tuft on the seed of willows. Bot.Mag. (Tokyo) 50, 283—289.

TAKHTAJAN, A., 1959: Evolution der Angiospermen. Jena: Fischer.

TAYLOR, B. W., 1954: An example of long-distance dispersal. Ecology 35, 569—572.

THELLUNG, A., 1930: Die Entstehung der Kulturpflanzen. München: Naturw. u. Landw.

THOMPSON, A. L., and R. E. MOREAU, 1957: Feeding habits of the palm-nut vulture. Ibis 99, 608—613.

THOMSON, R. B., 1927: Evolution of the seed habit in plants. Trans.R.Soc.Canada (V, 3d ser.) 20, 229—272.

TÜXEN, R. (edit.). 1966: Anthropogene Vegetation. Intern.Symp.Stolzenau 1961. The Hague: Junk.

ULBRICH, E., 1928: Biologie der Früchte und Samen (Karpobiologie). Berlin: Springer.

ULE, E., 1905: Wechselbeziehungen zwischen Ameisen und Pflanzen. Flora 94, 491—497.

UPHOF, J. C. TH., 1942: Ecological relations of plants with ants and termites. Bot. Review 8, 563—598.

DE VLAMING, V. and V. PROCTOR, 1968: Dispersal of aquatic orgnisms: viability of seeds recovered from the droppings of captive kildeer and mallard ducks. Amer. J.Bot 55, 20—26

WEBER, H., 1967: Vegetative Fortpflanzung bei Spermatophyten. In: Handbook of plant physiology, Vol. 18. Berlin-Heidelberg-New York: Springer.

WEIGELT, J., 1930: Über die vermutliche Nährung von Protorosaurus. Leopoldina 6, 269—280.

WENT, F. W., 1949: Ecology of desert plants, II. Ecology 30, 1—13.

WHITEHEAD, M. R., and C. A. BROWN, 1940: The seed of the spider lily, Hymeno-callis occidentalis. Amer.J.Bot. 27, 199—303.

WINKLER, H., 1939/40: Versuch eines „natürlichen" Systems der Früchte. Beitr.Biol. Pflanzen 26, 201—220; 27, 92—130, 242—267.

ZAZHURILO, C., 1940: (Russian title). On the anatomy of the seed coat of the Magnoliaceae (Liriodendron tulipifera L.). Bjull.Voron.Obcs.est. 4 (1), 32—40.

ZIMMERMANN, W., 1959: Die Phylogenie der Pflanzen. Stuttgart.

ZOHARY, M., 1937: Die verbreitungsökologischen Verhältnisse der Pflanzen Palästinas, I. Beih.Bot.Zbl. A 56, 1—155.

—, 1939: Karpobiologische Beiträge aus der orientalischen Flora. Botan. Notizer 1939, 528.

—, 1948: Carpological studies in Cruciferae. Palest.J.Bot.Jerusalem 4, 158—165.

—, 1950: Evolutionary trends in the fruiting head of Compositae. Evolution 4, 103—109.

Subject Index

Including vernacular names of plants and animals

lomentum 65, 126
lotos 64, 99

macrobiocarpy 83
mammals 39
mangrove 95
megasporangium 104
megaspores 103
megaspermy 108
migration 4, 6
migrule 8
mimesis 36
mimicry 36
mistle-thrush 26
mole rats 12
monkeys 46
monospermy 16, 109, 121
monovuly 16, 109
mountain-tops 89
mucilage (on seeds) 94
multiple fruit 9
myrmecochory 47, 117
myxospermy 61, 62, 84, 94

nautohydrochory 61
nomads 91, 98
nut-cracker 26
nutmeg 30, 116

oak 27, 99
obturator 116
oil-bird 33
oil-fruits 33, 47
oil-palm 33
olive 33
ombrohydrochory 62, 103
opportunists 98
ornithochory 25
osmotic pressure 96
ovule 107

pacu 21
pagoda-structure 43
palisade-layer 13, 112, 117, 119
panther 46
pappus 17, 49, 56, 60, 66, 68, 73, 78
parasites 48, 55, 93
peccary 41
pericarp-fruit 118
pest-pressure 85
pigeons 26, 30

piracanjuba 21
placenta-pulp 118
ploidy-level 132, 133
polychory 80
position 15
precinctiveness 90
precision-dispersal 48, 93
presentation 2, 58, 61, 70, 100
propagule 8
pseudocarp 9
pseudo-funicle 111, 115, 118
pseudo-hilum 115
pseudo-vivipary 10
pulpa 117, 126

quince 42

rain-ballists 62
rain-forest 85
rain-wash 62, 84
recolonisation 86
rejuvenation 87
reptiles 22, 105
ricinolic acid 49
rinnenhülse 62
river-transport 65
rodents 39
rose of Jericho 58
ruminants 40, 42, 127

sacrifice of dispersal 105, 108
samara 57
sapucaja-nut 45
saprophytes 55
sarcotesta 22, 31, 37, 40, 106, 110
saurochory 21
sclerochores 8
scobiform seeds 55
sea-currents 65
secondary forest 87
seed-habit 104
seedling-flotation 63
seedling-waiting 87, 98
shake-burrs 68
shore plants 65, 91, 95
shift of functions 102
size of diaspores 55, 76, 87, 108
smell 23, 30, 41, 43
snails 20
sociology 91
speciation 49, 81
spininess 69

Index of Scientific Plant Names

Reference to vernacular names in the Subject Index.
Numbers in *italics* refer to illustrations

Index of Scientific Animal Names

Reference to vernacular names in the subject index

Herstellung: Konrad Triltsch, Graphischer Betrieb, Würzburg

DATE DUE